Café Brosse

A comedy

Jean McConnell

Samuel French — London
www.samuelfrench-london.co.uk

Originally performed, under the title *Chord On the Triangle*, on BBC Radio, and subsequently published by H.F.W. Deane in 1961, copyright Jean McConnell 1961.

CHARACTERS

George, proprietor of the Café Brosse
Seraphine, George's wife
Yvette, George's mistress
Aramis, George's best friend
Aunt Marie, George's wealthy aunt
Raymond, a regular customer
Male Foreigner } *These parts may be played*
Female Foreigner } *by two women or two men*

The setting throughout is a café in a small town in
rural France

Time: the present

SYNOPSIS OF SCENES

Act I
SCENE 1 Early afternoon in the Café Brosse
SCENE 2 Late evening, a few days later

Act II
SCENE 1 Morning, one week later
SCENE 2 Midday, two weeks later

COPYRIGHT INFORMATION

(See also page ii)

This play is fully protected under the Copyright Laws of the British Commonwealth of Nations, the United States of America and all countries of the Berne and Universal Copyright Conventions.

All rights including Stage, Motion Picture, Radio, Television, Public Reading, and Translation into Foreign Languages, are strictly reserved.

Licences for amateur performances are issued subject to the understanding that it shall be made clear in all advertising matter that the audience will witness an amateur performance; that the names of the authors of the plays shall be included on all programmes; and that the integrity of the authors' work will be preserved.

The Royalty Fee is subject to contract and subject to variation at the sole discretion of Samuel French Ltd.

In theatres or halls seating four hundred or more the fee will be subject to negotiation.

In territories overseas the fee quoted above may not apply. A fee will be quoted on application to our local authorized agent, or if there is no such agent, on application to Samuel French Ltd, London.

VIDEO-RECORDING OF AMATEUR PRODUCTIONS

ACT I

Scene 1

A café in a small French town. Early afternoon

R is the bar and behind it an arch with bead curtain leads to the kitchen. Above the bar a staircase. UL is a door to a cupboard and DL a door to the cellar. Downstage are a few tables and chairs. Upstage is the main entrance, and outside can be glimpsed tables and chairs set for customers. The whole place has a sunny cheerful aspect

At the opening of the play, Seraphine stands at the open door U gazing out moodily. She is neither sunny nor cheerful right now. The radio is playing. She comes down and flicks at the tables with a tea-towel. Then she goes behind the bar, switches off the radio and leans on the counter with a melancholy sigh

George, her husband, enters from the cellar with bottles of wine under his arms. He is a good-natured, unassuming man. Humming to himself he crosses to the bar and dumps down the bottles

Seraphine gives an angry cry

George is startled

Seraphine flourishes the tea-towel at him

Seraphine George! Look what you are doing – scratching the polish to pieces! (*She thrusts the bottles back at him*)
George I am not——
Seraphine Scratching it to pieces! Look! Here and here——
George I didn't do that!
Seraphine I tell you, you have just this minute done it! Look at it! Scratched to pieces!
George Scratched to pieces! Just the smallest mark!
Seraphine All of them are small until there are enough of them—and

then you have a big mark! (*She rubs at it with the tea-towel*)

George All right! I have made a mark!

Seraphine On that beautiful surface!

George And who made the beautiful surface? Me! I polish it, so who is allowed to make a mark if not me!

Seraphine Of course, if you don't care whether we run a high-class café or a back-alley soup kitchen why should I worry! (*She flounces to the main door again, folds her arms and stares out even more dejectedly*)

George places the bottles down on the bar with elaborate care

George (*following Seraphine*) Seraphine, please! Aren't we partners? Don't we work together? (*Anxiously*) what is the matter? You used to sing about the place. Heaven knows you've no voice but it was cheerful. I thought you were happy—but lately…

Seraphine Happy—huh!

George Is the place getting you down? Are you working too hard?

Seraphine I can work you off your feet!

George I know you can. Well, if it's not that——

Seraphine (*turning to George*) How long have we been married, George?

George Nearly fifteen years, I think. Yes, it must be, because the year after we moved in here Madame Gorgette's tank burst and swamped my wedding suit I'd hung in the landing cupboard because you were spring-cleaning—and then we lent it to Alexis who caught pneumonia—and he's been dead at least fourteen years——

Seraphine Fifteen years! Fifteen years—and what have I got out of it? Take my hand!

George Now, Seraphine, you know I love you and——

Seraphine Take my hand, I said.

George wipes his hands on his apron and takes Seraphine's hand

You feel? Like an old brick wall. Red and rough and worn out!

George (*worried*) Yes, it is, isn't it? (*Examining it with growing distaste*) Couldn't you get some cream or something?

Seraphine It's not just my hands! It's all of me!

George Now, come Seraphine, you're not red and rough all over—why I was only thinking the other day——

Seraphine I am worn out, George!

George Nonsense, my dear, you've years to go yet.

Seraphine (*moving* D) Yes! Years of working by your side in the bar all day! Eating our meals—you one end of the table—I the other.

Sweeping up the place at night. Going to bed—one-third for me—two-thirds for you—fighting for the blankets! Waking in the morning beside a piece of green suet—breathing through its mouth. (*She sits down* R)

George (*following Seraphine* D) A piece of—you mean me?

Seraphine Open the shutters—swab the floor—and hail to another day! Like yesterday—and the day before—and tomorrow and the day after——

George Seraphine! You're not yourself!

Seraphine Ha! But I am. That's the trouble. I am Seraphine—wife of George, proprietor of the café in the square in Saladup, Department·of Drome, France! Would you wish anyone such a fate? (*Sighing gustily*) I am going to make some coffee.

George We have just had some coffee. It is time to open the shutters again.

Seraphine Open them yourself! (*She rises and moves to the bar*)

George Oh, very well, but what about the floor? A fine old mess Jacques made at lunchtime—just look!

Seraphine I'll get you a bucket. (*She goes behind the bar*)

George Seraphine!

Seraphine (*mocking*) Seraphine!

George Seraphine, what have I done? Why are you angry with me? Very well, I will wash the floor. I have always tried to be a good husband. Have I not been a good husband?

Seraphine Yes. (*She leans across the bar despondently*)

George Well, and I will go on being one. And you have been a good wife, Seraphine.

Seraphine That's the point, I don't want to go on being one. I'm sick and tired of being one. Fifteen years is long enough in any situation—especially when it's a dead end.

George (*crossing to the bar*) Seraphine! You wouldn't leave me?

Seraphine Certainly, if I could think of somewhere better to go—but I can't at the moment. It's very aggravating!

George But you can't do that! You mean everything to me! How could I live without you? And you know very well you haven't got the book-keeping up to date!

Seraphine I could do that in less than an hour if the necessity arose.

Seraphine exits to the kitchen

George gives a bewildered shrug and puts the bottles on the shelves. He then examines the counter surface

George (*sighing*) Tch, tch, tch. Scratched to pieces. (*He moves U and begins opening the shutters*)

Aramis enters. He is dressed in a cream linen suit, panama and carrying a case; with a buttonhole and cane he is the complete sophisticate—or so he believes. His voice is fruity, even pompous, but his affection for George is genuine. He is carrying a case and a paper bag of pastries

Aramis (*shaking George's hand*) Good afternoon, my dear George. How are we this afternoon?

George Ah, good afternoon, Aramis. So-so. So-so. You are early.

Aramis Yes. I am taking a little work home. I need quiet and in the office, you know how it is, telephone calls, decisions, queries—at every-one's beck and call.

George You shouldn't be so efficient!

Aramis Well, there it is. May I place my pastries on the counter?

George Certainly. (*Shutters complete, he goes behind the bar*)

Aramis And I wonder——

George (*anticipating*) Of course! My wife is just making some coffee. At least I think so. (*Calling through the arch*) My dear. Aramis is here! Coffee for him, if you please. (*He waits—there is no reply. He sighs, but remains hopeful*) It will be out in a minute.

Aramis Splendid. (*He moves DL*)

George (*to himself*) I hope.

Aramis George! George, come here. I want to show you what I got in the post this morning.

George joins him and Aramis produces a stamp from a small transparent envelope

George A ten-centime black. The very stamp you wanted, eh?

Aramis What do you think of that?

George (*taking a small magnifying glass from his pocket and examining the stamp*) What a beauty. Congratulations!

Aramis (*producing a similar glass and gazing also*) Ten years I have been waiting for it—ten years!

George Fortunate man.

They are both lost in admiration

Seraphine makes an irritable exclamation in the kitchen

George's face clouds

Aramis reverently places the stamp back in the envelope

Aramis And George, I also have something for you.
George Oh?
Aramis Here. A blue Mauritius! I have another now—so you can have this one to complete your set. (*He hands it to George*)
George That's very nice of you.
Aramis (*expecting a bigger reaction*) You wanted it didn't you?
George Yes, yes. Thank you. (*He pockets the stamp and moves to the bar. He begins placing the pastries on a plate*)
Aramis Well, I thought you would be more excited.
George Oh, I am—inside—you know. It just isn't showing. It's the weather, you know.
Seraphine (*off*) George!
George (*starting*) Ah! That's Seraphine. (*Moving to the arch*) This'll be your coffee.
Aramis Excellent! (*He sits L of the table LC*)
Seraphine (*thrusting a bucket through the arch*) The bucket!

George takes the bucket

George The bucket. (*He moves to Aramis, plate in one hand, bucket in the other*)
Aramis I'd sooner have it in a cup.
George (*laughing uneasily*) This is for the floor. The coffee will follow—I expect. Do you mind if I swab round you? That Jacques—spilt a whole bottle—and that rot-gut he drinks would take the pattern off a carpet. (*He gets a mop from the cupboard—replacing a broom which falls out*)
Aramis Go ahead, my dear fellow. I will sit and watch. That is always a pleasant feeling, eh?
George Yes, indeed. (*He puts his hand in the water and draws it out with a gasp of pain. He turns crossly towards the arch then thinks better of it. He begins swabbing with gusty sighs*)
Aramis (*eating*) I pride myself that I am a particularly observant man, mm—excuse me—these pastries—delicious! But were I the most insensitive creature alive I could hardly fail to realize that something is amiss with you.
George No, no, I am quite well.
Aramis My dear George, you can't deceive me. Are we not old friends? I am a man of the world, George—of experience—of discretion, George. Come, get it off your chest.
George (*giving in*) You're right of course, Aramis. You're a very perceptive man.

Aramis I know life, George, I know people.

George   Aramis, I need your advice. (*He joins Aramis at the table, sitting* R)

Aramis Only too glad to help.

George I appeal to you. I'm in great trouble.

Aramis My dear fellow.

George I have been married for fifteen years

Aramis Yes—well—that's enough for anyone, I suppose.

George No, no, I'm not complaining about that.

Aramis   I would be! Marriage—ah! A condition I'd never relish myself.

George Oh, it's not me. The trouble is that my wife has lately become quite terribly dissatisfied and restless.

Aramis Oh, George, how well I understand. It's so usual, dear fellow, so usual. I've seen it often. Fifteen, twenty years of comparative calm and then a great fog of discontent descends over the little woman. She becomes petulant, unhappy——

George Yes!

Aramis Depressed, edgy, miserable, nervous—altogether a pathetic little figure.

George Yes, yes.

Aramis Oh, I know the symptoms. They're very distressing. And in the circumstances there is obviously only one course an intelligent husband can take.

George And that is?

Aramis Find consolation elsewhere.

George Oh, but——

Aramis   Yes! Acquire for himself a sympathetic young feminine companion.

George But——

Aramis Isn't it a splendid notion now? Of course, it may come as a shock to you, but take my advice, as a man of the world—take to your bosom—to put it crudely—some enchanting creature who will console you.

George It's no good, Aramis, I can't do that.

Aramis Why ever not?

George Because I already have.

Aramis (*startled*) I beg your pardon?

George I said—I already have. Her name's Yvette. I keep her in a basement in Place Napoleon.

Aramis George, I had no idea—I mean, you've never said a word.

George It was five years ago, at least. I was feeling depressed, edgy, miserable and nervous at the time and it cheered me up no end.

Aramis Well, you dark old horse! But there you are, old fellow, there's your answer, don't you see.

George But I couldn't possibly afford another one!

Aramis No, no, no! What an idea! Bluebeard! You just give your wife a little hint about her—and she'll be back at your feet before you can turn round. Nothing like a little competition to bring a woman up to scratch. Take my word for it. Just you let her know!

George But she does know, Aramis.

Aramis What?

George Yes. I told her. I'd never do anything without consulting my wife.

Aramis But—but—didn't she mind?

George No. She said it was all right, just so long as she knew where I was.

Aramis Mm. Are you sure she heard what you said?

George Oh yes. She's always been a good-natured woman. And I put it to her very diplomatically, mind. Once she was assured it would make no financial difference, she said she didn't mind a bit, if it kept me out of mischief. In fact she'd be glad to have me off her hands from time to time.

Aramis Well, I must say, you and Seraphine have hidden the situation very successfully.

George Well, we've all been perfectly happy, you see, and Place Napoleon is rather off the beaten track.

Aramis My dear fellow—it's miles.

George The exercise was good for me too. Yes, we were all right until these last few months, when Seraphine has suddenly become moody. Really, she's making life unbearable.

Aramis But we're back where we started, George, don't you see? Fly to the arms of—what was it?—Yvette! She should comfort you.

George She should—but you see she's been so very depressed, edgy, miserable and nervous lately that——

Aramis My dear George!

George You see, Aramis, I have something of a problem.

Aramis I grant you, George, you have a problem.

George I love them, Aramis. I want them to be happy. As it is, I leave a disgruntled face and harsh word here, only to meet a harsh face and a disgruntled word in Place Napoleon. Poor darlings, they are eating their hearts out. And I am leading the life of a ping-pong ball. (*He rises, walks to the bar and leans there disconsolately*)

Aramis I appreciate your dilemma.

George What do you advise?

Aramis It's tricky. You must leave it to me. But don't worry, something will come. Women, my dear George, follow a set pattern—like Fair Isle cardigans. Scotland you know.

George Ah, Aramis, I rely on your experience. A travelled man has a deeper understanding of human nature, I always think. I consider myself fortunate to be——   .

Two Foreigners, carrying brushes, are seen passing outside

Oh, excuse me! There is someone waiting outside the café. (*He hastily stows away the bucket and mop in the cupboard*)

Aramis Oh? No, no, George, they've passed on.

George So they have. And whether they'll get coffee if they want it Seraphine only knows. (*He sighs*)

Aramis Here, George, to cheer you up. I was taking this stamp to Father Michel, but you shall have it. A 1929 two-franc brown!

George How kind you are. I must settle with you.

Aramis Yes. I would offer it as a gift, George, but it doesn't do, you know. Once we started that you wouldn't be free to ask me to get special stamps for you, would you?

George That's true.

Aramis And I would begin keeping news of such finds from you in case you didn't expect to pay. I tell you, our relationship would be ruined.

George You always understand human nature so well. Thanks for the stamp. Will this see us square? (*He hands notes to Aramis*)

Aramis Thank you. Take this one back. I want no commission.

The Foreigners with brushes cross again

George You are a good friend. Ah! Here come that couple again. I must go and dust the tables. Excuse me, Aramis.

George goes out

Aramis (*to himself*) Ah dear! Poor man—what a predicament. But a little friend—in Place Napoleon—what about that?

Seraphine enters through the arch carrying a cup of coffee

Seraphine Good afternoon, Aramis.

Aramis (*rising and shaking Seraphine's hand*) Seraphine, my dear girl, how are you?

Seraphine (*wearily*) Here is your coffee, Aramis. (*She sits R of Aramis' table, gazing moodily out front*) Oh! Aramis I'm far from bright this afternoon.

Aramis Come now, Seraphine, why is a fortunate woman like you so depressed. (*He sinks his teeth into a large pastry*)

Seraphine Fortunate? How fortunate? Do you know how old I am?

Aramis (*treading on eggs*) Er—um—twe—er—thir—uh—you are a child, my dear.

Seraphine I am thirty-five, Aramis.

Aramis Age, what is age? You are a sweet, inexperienced girl.

Seraphine Only for want of opportunity, Aramis! And anyway, don't you be so certain.

Aramis Oh, Seraphine, everyone knows what a loyal wife you are.

Seraphine And what's so splendid about that? Who gets the chance to kick over the traces in Saladup. Look out of the window, Aramis. What a place! Brooms, brushes, wherever you look.

Aramis Well, of course, it is the local industry. We make excellent brooms and brushes here. We are proud of it, aren't we?

Seraphine I'm sick of it.

Aramis What's wrong with it?

Seraphine Every shop—every place—crammed full of them—every shape and size. They sprout from every nook and cranny—like a housewife's nightmare!

Aramis A good brush is a good friend.

Seraphine My epitaph, Aramis: "She swept clean to the last."

Aramis Oh come, it's the same elsewhere. What about Montelimar. Have you been there?

Seraphine You know I haven't.

Aramis I can tell you—the whole place is devoted to nougat. Every shop, every bar sells it. Every inch of space on the walls advertises it. I ask you? Imagine living there—especially if you haven't a sweet tooth. (*He takes another mammoth bite*)

Seraphine I don't care about Montelimar. I am concerned with this place. And anyway, it's not just the place, it's my life. Aramis, I am at the end of my tether. Sometimes I wish I had run away to Paris when I was sixteen like Jeanne Ory who went to the bad—lucky thing!

Aramis Now, now, now—I understand.

Seraphine Oh, I am so fed up! Lately this nice little café feels like a cage round me. When I walk down the street, the brooms seem to be pointing at me from the shops! And poor George, so kind, so willing to please. I am sure before long I am going to murder him.

Aramis I should try not to do that. At least not until I've thought the problem over. It's natural for a woman of your spirit and intelligence to dream—but you mustn't do anything hasty.

Seraphine You're such a wise man, Aramis—so unlike George, who hasn't the first notion what goes on in a woman's head.

Seraphine rises and moves behind the bar as George is heard approaching

Well, here he comes now. Customers too. Coffee wanted, I suppose. (*Calling*) Coffee, George?

George enters, followed by the Foreigners (still carrying brushes), and moves downstage

George I don't know. Wait a minute. (*Calling*) Come this way, please! (*Aside*) Aramis, you must help us, I can't understand a word they are saying. (*He shepherds the couple* C)

Aramis (*rising*) Oh? Foreigners? Where from?

George That's just it. I can't discover. I've tried English and German. Have a go will you? You're good at languages.

Aramis (*moving* L *of the Foreigners*) Well, I—er—good afternoon sir— madam!

Male Foreigner (*with difficulty*) Goot afternoon.

George I got that far.

Aramis Did you try American?

George No.

Aramis *Cawfy, bub?*

Male Foreigner Uh?

George That's no good.

Aramis Bitte, wollen sie—oh, you tried that. Er—*què piensan usted enel tiempo?* That's Spanish.

Seraphine What did you ask them?

Aramis I asked them what they thought of the weather.

George That's going to get us a long way.

Aramis They obviously don't understand anyway. (*He moves* DL)

Seraphine (*going* C) Wait a minute. Let me try. (*Enunciating*) Good afternoon.

George Again?

Seraphine Coffee, eh? (*She makes a drinking noise*) Mm? Sip, sip, sip! Mm? Yes? (*She makes more sucking noises*)

Both Foreigners (*eagerly affirmative*) Mmm! Mmm! Mmm!

Seraphine There. At least we know they are thirsty. I'll get them some coffee.

Seraphine goes off into the kitchen

George (*indicating the table* R) Sit! Sit!

The Foreigners stare uncomprehendingly

Aramis Sit! Sit!

As Aramis and George seat themselves at the table to demonstrate, the Foreigners promptly begin to wander dismally off. George and Aramis leap up, seize them, and place them in the chairs at the table DR

Foreigners (*making noisy chewing sounds*) Yum yum yum!
George I think they are hungry too. I'll get some pastries from the bakers.

Seraphine enters, and moves DR

Aramis (*furtively offering his plate to George*) Here, use these, I don't want any more of them.

Surreptitiously George passes the plate to Seraphine

George (*hissing*) Take these to the kitchen.
Seraphine (*taking the plate*) All right. (*Moving off*) Well, that's that.

Seraphine goes out through the arch

Male Foreigner Um.
Aramis I think he wants to tell you something, George.
George (*crossing* R) Oh dear. Yes, sir?
Male Foreigner Brrrrrrrr. (*He mimes driving*)
George (*startled*) Whatever's the matter with him?
Aramis I think he's supposed to be a motor-car.
George Oh.
Male Foreigner (*eagerly*) Mm. Mm. Car! Brrr-pht! Pht! Phew!
George Eh?
Female Foreigner Bbrrrrrrrr-pht! Pht! Phut!
Aramis They broke down.
George Have they been to a garage?
Male Foreigner (*affirmatively*) Mmm. Garage!
Aramis They have.

Male Foreigner holds up his finger

George What's he doing now—point up in the air?
Aramis He's telling us, "One".
George "One" what? One pastry?
Male Foreigner Un un brrrrrrr! (*He mimes looking under car bonnet, shaking head sadly and holding his finger up again*)
Aramis No, I think he means it's going to take "One" something to mend the car.

George One hour, I suppose.

Aramis Wonder where they are from?

George Try some other languages, Aramis.

Aramis (*hastily*) It's not worth it. They're obviously not Europeans or they'd know *some* French.

George He's making more signs, Aramis. Whatever do they want now? Aramis what do they mean?

Aramis What's the matter, madam?

Aramis and George close in, standing downstage of the Foreigners' table, backs to the audience. Female Foreigner can be heard grunting and gasping. Suddenly enlightened, George and Aramis break L

George (*taking Female Foreigner upstage*) Straight upstairs, madam.

Female Foreigner goes upstairs

Aramis What a mime! Well, George, I must be off.

George You spoke to Seraphine?

Aramis picks up his case, stick and hat

Aramis Yes. Things are certainly black, old friend, but don't despair. I'll bear it in mind and call back.

George Please do. I need your support. I swear I cannot go on like this. I'd do anything for her—anything.

Aramis See you later, George. (*Moving off*) Good day, sir.

Male Foreigner Uh-uh. Good—er pf!

George (*coming down to Male Foreigner*) Nice brushes you have there.

Male Foreigner Brutzi. Mm.

George Brushes. Yes.

Male Foreigner (*nodding and smiling*) Brutzi! Brutzi!

George (*nodding and smiling*) Yes, yes, brushes, yes.

Male Foreigner Brutzi.

George Brushes. Mm. (*He walks away and clears Aramis' cup*) Well, that's established.

Seraphine enters, carrying a tray with two cups of coffee and a plate of pastries

Seraphine Here is the coffee.

George takes the tray off her and places on the table R

George Ah! Your coffee, sir.
Male Foreigner Ah! Ha! Ha!

Female Foreigner comes downstairs

Female Foreigner (*returning to the table*) Peretzi caren posn arech, voob.
Male Foreigner Er—um—sip sip—ugh! (*He grimaces*)
Seraphine (*interpreting*) Sugar, George, sugar! (*She hands George a bowl*)
George (*giving it to the Foreigners*) Sugar. Mm? Ah!

The Foreigners make weird grunts of gratitude

George gives them an enormous smile, then turns back to Seraphine with a grimace

Charming! (*He switches on the radio and bright music starts up*)

George starts to exit into the cellar

Raymond enters the main door. He is a working man and is waving the sports section of a newspaper. He is slightly drunk

Raymond George! Now this will settle the argument! Look here! (*He flourishes the newspaper at George*) Now tell me what do you think of Carfechot! Twenty-seventh!
George Carfechot? He's not done so well this season I'll grant.
Raymond Right! Right!
George But he hasn't lost his touch.
Raymond Lost his touch! He never had a touch. Never rated! Dead loss that Carfechot! Couldn't ride a skate-board.

Seraphine pours Raymond a drink in a small glass, obviously his usual. Raymond downs the drink and as Seraphine passes, he tries to waltz her to the music. She pushes him aside. Raymond waltzes on alone. Seraphine examines the bottles George brought from the cellar

Seraphine What on earth have you brought up from the cellar, George!
George (*to Raymond*) Just an unfortunate fluke? Have you ever studied Carfechot in action? Have you?
Raymond Couldn't ride a scooter.

George What are you talking about, Raymond? How often have you seen him anyway?

Raymond Couldn't ride a penny farthing!

George No, no, no! Have you ever seen him? Ever?

Raymond Ccouldn't ride a donkey!

George I admit he didn't do well last season but it was that bicycle – all the fault of that machine.

Seraphine (*to George*) Why do you always bring up the opposite of what I have asked for!

George What do you mean, Seraphine? What is the opposite of Vin Ordinaire? Champagne? Did you want that?

Seraphine Oh, don't be stupid!

Raymond Couldn't ride a cock-horse!

George (*to Raymond*) Anyone could see it was the cycle holding him back. It was not a good one.

Raymond Would have done better on skates! (*His dancing turns to skating*)

George Carfechot has been very good. On and off!

Raymond Off I agree with.

George I tell you he's got style. It's in the shoulders and arms – haven't you noticed. Look, this is him. (*He crouches over an imaginary racing cycle*)

Raymond Couldn't ride a perambulator.

Raymond waltzes George, George extricates himself

George Now if you were talking about Duplessis!

Raymond Ah, but it's all in the calves with him. Only rides with his legs.

George Now you're talking legs! A star!

Raymond But Carfechot? They'll never be any more use to him. Not as legs that is.

George Have it your way.

The Foreigners rise. Raymond invites them to dance. Flustered, they push money at George

  The Foreigners exit

George Good-day sir – madam!

Seraphine George! I distinctly said brandy.

George Did you?

Seraphine You have only to look at the bottle!

George I should have noticed.

Seraphine You never notice anything! (*She turns off the radio*)

Seraphine exits upstairs

George Why, that's not true Seraphine, I——
Raymond If my wife spoke to me like that I'd clip her round the ear.
George No, no, Raymond. She is just a little on edge.
Raymond All I can say is if my wife spoke to me like that I'd hit her with a chair.
George Yes, yes, Raymond. Get off to work now.
Ramond All I can say is—if my wife spoke to me like that I'd take hold of her by the hair and swing her round and round my head and throw her against the wall. She'd think twice next time.
George All I can say is it's a blessing you're a bachelor. Come on! Cheerio! (*He drags Raymond upstage*)
Raymond I'd wring her neck like a skinny little pullet!
George (*to himself*) A good fellow really.

Seraphine comes downstairs, with a shawl on

Seraphine Will you watch out, George, I'm going for a stroll.
George Seraphine, stay and talk to me for a while. You've hardly spoken to me all day.
Seraphine What is there to talk about, the price of coffee? Did you order more Anisette? What an amusing life we lead.
George (*moving* U) Oh now, Seraphine, there you go again. Would you like a new dress?
Seraphine Yes.
George Then take a little something out of the till, my dear.
Seraphine (*exasperatedly*) Oh, you just don't understand. (*She moves to the door where she pauses*) Huh! Those two foreigners are wandering round the square like a pair of lost shoes.
George (*following her gaze off*) Dear, dear, poor things.
Seraphine At least they're having a change!

Aramis approaches from R *and enters*

George Hallo, Aramis. Come in, old friend.
Aramis (*following their gaze*) Looking at those foreigners? Pierre at the garage and his wife have talked to them. He says they're from Reykjavik and on their way to visit old friends in Hyeres. Although his wife declares they said they were Estonians going to a business conference in Lisbon. Either way they've had to send for a spare part for the car, so they're stuck here.

George They're setting themselves up all right for brushes, I see.

Seraphine What else could they do in this town?

Aramis It's good for trade I suppose.

Seraphine I bet they give them all away. She doesn't look the type who drudges in the home all day.

George Oh, Seraphine, all you can talk about is how you slave in the house. Well, some people would like the chance, so there.

Seraphine I don't believe it—who?

George Never mind—there are some.

Seraphine Oh, how like you! I'm not staying to listen to such nonsense.

Seraphine strides off, exiting UL

Aramis You mustn't say these things, George. You only provoke her more.

George But it's true.

Aramis Now come, George, what sort of woman would——

George Yvette—that's the sort! (*He moves* DC)

Aramis (*following George*) Who's Yvette? Oh, Yvette.

George Yes, Yvette. She does nothing but complain because she's not an ordinary housewife.

Aramis Does she indeed. Mm. Look here, George, suppose we pop along and see her. Is that possible?

George Of course. Believe me it will be no fun here with Seraphine. As soon as Seraphine returns we'll go. But what have you in mind?

Aramis Just the germ of an idea, George, the merest germ.

George I'll get myself tidied up. One puts on a tie you know, Aramis.

Aramis Naturally. (*He sits at the bar on a stool*)

George (*starting to prepare himself, taking his tie from the pegs behind the bar*) The address is number twelve, the riverside of sixteen, Place Napoleon.

Aramis Well! I've passed that house a hundred times and more.

George Oh, the house is nothing to do with us, we go round the back and down to a basement flat. (*He crosses to a mirror on the wall* L)

Aramis What a romantic little love-nest and on the riverside. Perfect!

George One goes down a few stone steps and then there is a yellow door.

Aramis Charming. (*He crosses to George; conspiratorally*) You have a special knock?

George (*affronted*) Certainly not! No one else comes there, Aramis.

Aramis Of course not. I do apologize. Of course, you have a key? (*He sits* C)

George Naturally, but I always knock first—just to give her a moment to prepare herself.

Aramis How thoughtful. That's the way.

George She's a charming child, Aramis. Mind, she may not be to your taste.

Aramis They are all to my taste, George.

George (*crossing to the coat-pegs*) And yet you never got tied up with one. What an ingenious man you are! (*He puts on his coat*)

Aramis I understand them, George. I know how to handle them. When you've had the experience I've had, you get to know the traps. Anyone can get through the front door, George—it's knowing how to make a dignified exit out the same way. No scurrying down the back stairs for me.

George Then inside there is a tiny hall—bijou you know.

Aramis (*deeply envious*) Who needs more?

George And I call—Yvette! I call—and there is no reply.

Aramis No reply?

George No reply. And do you know why?

Aramis She's out.

George No, no, no. She's hiding. I have to find her.

Aramis Oh, I see. Delightful.

George I pretend not to for a while of course—although frankly I know most of the places by now, but she enjoys it, you know. Then at last out she pops and we curl up on the rug in front of the stove and have a delicious little cup of chocolate.

Aramis What a paradise.

George Rather pleasant.

Aramis (*rising*) I must say I'd never have guessed.

George and Aramis move U

George (*as they go*) Yvette has a highly developed sense of responsibility, Aramis. She's discreet. I've never had a moment's cause for embarrassment.

Yvette appears in the doorway

George turns and sees Yvette

Yvette!

Yvette enters. She is in her twenties or so—normally pleasant, but at present in a thunderous mood

Aramis Yvette?

Yvette *Yes!*

George What are you doing here?

Yvette I wanted to see you.

George But I was just on my way to you. What are you thinking of, coming here? (*To Aramis*) She's never done such a thing before.

Yvette There's a first time for everything. (*She sits R of the table LC*)

George (*following Yvette D*) But, Yvette, it's not in good taste and what is more——

Aramis (*snapping his fingers at George and moving DL*) George! George!

George Eh? Oh, I beg your pardon. Yvette, this is Aramis—you've heard me speak of him.

Yvette How do you do?

Aramis Enchanted. (*He shakes her hand and sits U of the table LC*)

George Happily, Seraphine has just gone out.

Yvette I know, I saw her.

George (*mollified*) Oh. (*To Aramis*) You see? Considerate. (*Taking Yvette's hand*) My little pet. I do apologize for giving you such a boorish greeting.

Yvette That's all right.

George You're looking sweeter than ever.

Yvette Well, I'm not feeling it.

George I was just telling Aramis about our jolly times together. How you always hide from me—you little tease! As if I won't find you.

Yvette Well, it was your damn silly idea for me to do it—and if you don't imagine I've exhausted the possibilities of that shoe box of a flat—!

George Sh, sh, sh! Yes, stupid of me.

Yvette (*rising*) George, you've got to get a builder in. There's water coming through the walls!

George Now, now, Yvette, you mustn't exaggerate. I know it's a little damp.

Yvette Damp! The steps are so slimy one of my friends slid from top to bottom.

George One of your friends?

Yvette Broke the heel of her shoe.

George (*relieved*) Oh. But, Yvette, that's the price one has to pay for being so close to the river. And what's a little watermark on the wallpaper here and there.

Yvette I tell you there is a distinct trickle of water—one can hear it.

George Tch—what an imagination. You must have left the tap running. Now confess, have you investigated properly?

Yvette Well, I——

George (*seating Yvette again*) There, little silly. Such a kitten. I'll get the walls papered again.

Yvette But you only had it done a few months ago.

George (*his brow creasing*) Yes. Never mind, think what fun you'll have choosing the paper.

Yvette It's not a bad idea. I'm certainly sick of those blue roses.

George (*for Aramis' benefit*) They were a very pretty pink before the damp came through.

Yvette (*gloomily*) How's Seraphine?

George Very well.

Yvette She would be.

George Yvette, please!

Yvette Who wouldn't be? Leading a normal life like her. Slopping round the place in comfy slippers and a warm dressing-gown while I have to wear those exasperating mules and a draughty négligé! She can enjoy cooking meals in that lovely big kitchen on a stove the size of a tar-boiler. She can tie her head up in a duster and clump round having a wonderful spring clean, while I'm expected to keep the place looking like a harem in satin and lace and stuff! (*Rising*) I tell you, George, I'm bored to the back teeth with loafing about, painted and powdered and scented and lacquered. My mind's getting as clogged as my pores. And if you want any more exotic little cups of chocolate made on that revolting gas ring, you can jolly well get them yourself! (*She sits*)

George (*sitting at the table* R; *sighing*) I was afraid you were getting fed up.

Aramis It's odd that you should envy Seraphine so much, because she's far from satisfied with her lot, you know.

Yvette Then she's a fool. What wouldn't I give just to have a normal home to run and ordinary behaviour to keep up.

George But that's just what Seraphine hates about it. She says it's dull.

Yvette Well, I wouldn't mind having a go, so there!

George (*miserably*) I'll get you a glass of Anisette. (*He moves behind the bar*)

Yvette (*to Aramis*) Poor George! He's been so good to me. But I'm sick of that poky little hole. I'd like to throw out that simpering nude over the mantelpiece and hang up a clock. I'd like to dump the joss-sticks and do the whole place over with disinfectant.

Aramis Now don't upset yourself, my dear.

George I'm afraid we're out of Anisette. (*He picks up a tea-towel*)

Yvette All right, I'll have disinfectant! Oh, George, I'm so miserable! (*She weeps*)

George (*kneeling beside her and mopping her tears with the tea-towel*)

There, there. We'll think of something, my precious. Well, Aramis?

Aramis (*rising and moving* U; *thoughtfully*) It's coming, George. It's coming. (*Starting*) Heavens, so is Seraphine!

Yvette Oh dear, I suppose I'd better go.

George Yes please. Cheer up, Yvette. I can't bear to see you unhappy.

Yvette Goodbye, George. (*She moves towards the door*)

George Sorry to hurry you away, Yvette, my pet, but Aramis has promised to help us out of our troubles.

Yvette If only he could.

Aramis I think I can. Yes, I think I can. Goodbye, Yvette.

George and Aramis, each kissing Yvette's hand, propel her out of the door

George, I have a splendid notion. It's quite clear how we can help Yvette, anyway, George. She's just dying to run your home for you. It should be easy enough to fix that, surely.

George How?

Aramis Send Seraphine away for a little while.

George You mean—

Aramis And let Yvette take her place.

George But—but I'd have to tell Seraphine.

Aramis Oh certainly! Nothing underhand I assure you.

George I wonder whether Seraphine would object?

Aramis (*glancing* U) Here she is, George. Ask her.

Seraphine enters U

George Seraphine, do listen, my dear, we've just had a splendid notion. I know how you've been feeling lately—how would you care for a little holiday?

Seraphine Holiday? What sort of a holiday?

Aramis You could go to a hotel—live in the lap of luxury and never even see a kitchen sink!

George You could go to Dijon! I have an aunt in Dijon—lives in a very smart hotel. Aunt Marie! She's never seen you, Seraphine, and she's always begging us to visit her. I have considerable expectations there, Aramis.

Seraphine Mm. I'd like to go away, it's true, but I don't know that I want to do as you say.

George But, Seraphine, what is your objection?

Seraphine It will be lonely.

George But you'll have Aunt Marie!

Seraphine How do I know I'll like her? I've never even seen her.
Aramis All the better. Think what a nice change it will be.
Seraphine I suppose so.
George Splendid. We'll get on the phone to Aunt Marie right away.
Seraphine I'd like to sleep on it.

Seraphine goes out through the arch

George (*with a groan*) That means we'll argue about it all night. (*Calling through the arch*) It's such a beautiful day for a trip, Seraphine! (*To Aramis*) I wonder if she'll go.
Aramis Of course she'll go. There! A little change for Yvette—a little holiday for Seraphine. Your troubles will soon be over.
George I'll phone Yvette. She'll be delighted anyway.
Aramis Phone your Aunt Marie first, George, that is the essential thing. I assure you.
George Yes, yes! You're right! What would I do without you Aramis.

George exits into the kitchen, through the arch

The Foreigners enter, laden with brooms and brushes

Aramis (*calling to George*) Leave them to me, George! (*To Male Forigner*) Hallo, sir, no car yet? No—brrr—yet?
Male Foreigner (*sadly*) Ah! Brrrr-beep-beep-brr-woomph!
Aramis Oh, I am sorry.

The Foreigners point upstage

You would like to sit outside? Certainly.

The Foreigners turn upstage, collide and drop their belongings

Seraphine looks out from the arch

I'd better help them with that lot. (*To the Foreigners*) Give me those brushes. Let me carry ——
Foreigners (*apprehensively*) Noh, noh, noh!
Aramis I'm only trying to assist you! Give me one——
Foreigners (*wildly*) Noh! Noh!
Aramis (*wrestling for the brushes*) Give me them — you silly old——

The Foreigners scream

Seraphine Better give up, Aramis. They don't understand.

The Foreigners gather up their possessions and hurry upstage and out of sight, where they are heard to drop the lot again

Aramis moves DL

Poor souls. What a motor tour they're having. (*She moves behind the bar and pours two glasses of wine and puts them on a tray*)
Aramis Tour? I understood they were going to a conference — or was it a visit to old friends?
Seraphine No, no, they told me at the post office. They are tourists from Tibet.
Aramis Oh, no, no. Ah, well, it doesn't matter. (*Taking the tray from Seraphine*) I'll take these out to them. (*He takes the tray* U)

George enters

George Good news! Aunt Marie says she will be happy to receive you, Seraphine. She hoped it wasn't catching.
Seraphine What wasn't catching?
George I told her you hadn't been well. Now, there's a train leaves for Dijon at eight-thirty tomorrow morning. Would you like me to help you pack?
Seraphine Yes, yes, time enough.
George I thought you were so anxious to get away from here.
Seraphine Not when you seem in such a hurry to get rid of me.
George Well, to be frank, Yvette's very anxious to come here as soon as possible.

Aramis returns

Seraphine (*coming* C) What nonsense. I can't imagine her rushing that hard to take up household chores. After all who in their right mind would want to give up her snug little existence — for this!
George I think she's quite looking forward to it.
Seraphine She must be mad. What woman wouldn't want her life. Lolling about in her best clothes all day with nothing to do but make herself pleasant.
Aramis Seraphine, are you serious?
Seraphine Of course I'm serious. I've always thought Yvette had much the better share of it. (*She sits* L *of the table* LC)
Aramis (*joining George* C) George—an idea has occurred to me. A

simply splendid idea!

George I—I don't know if it would work, Aramis.

Aramis Why not?

George No. No. Now, Seraphine, you will have to change at Brevey for Dijon and——

Aramis Dijon! Seraphine doesn't want to go there.

George (*firmly*) Yes she does!

Seraphine No I don't!

George Oh, Aramis! I almost got her on the train!

Aramis But, George, don't you see, she'll be so much happier in Place Napoleon.

Seraphine Place Napoleon—you mean?

Aramis Send her to Dijon, George, and she'll be back in two days. Why it'll be hardly any change at all—just a visit to relations. At Place Napoleon she can be someone else completely!

George No, no!

Seraphine (*going* c) Oh, George—I think it's a good idea!

George No!

Aramis And it will save money!

George (*hesitating*) There is that.

Seraphine No, I shall take the money just the same. I shall need different clothes. Imagine me in my jumpers and skirts. No, I shall want a lace wrapper and a gold lamé—and lots of pretty underwear! (*She twirls* u)

George (*following resentfully*) You never bought those for me.

Seraphine But I am buying them for you.

George Seraphine, dear, you will catch your death. It's not a very warm flat.

Seraphine It will be, George, I promise you. Aramis can take me over tomorrow first thing. I've never been there of course, Aramis.

George (*shocked*) Of course not.

Aramis Very well.

Seraphine (*seductively*) I shall expect you tomorrow night, George. Not too early mind—and don't forget I want to be treated exactly as you have always treated Yvette. Understand?

George Understood.

Seraphine I'll go and get my things together!

Seraphine exits upstairs

Aramis George, it couldn't be better!

George I'm not sure.

Aramis My dear fellow. Both the little girls will be happy and consequently they'll make you happy! (*He sits upstage of the table* LC)

George Do you think so? (*He brightens*)

Aramis Of course. I almost envy you.

George (*pouring drinks*) It's been very nice of you to take all this trouble, Aramis. (*He switches on the radio and music starts up*)

Aramis Rubbish. I know human nature, George. There is always a solution if real wisdom and understanding can be brought to bear.

George (*bringing drinks to the table and sitting* R *of the table* LC) What a weight you've taken off my mind!

Aramis I'll just look in tomorrow and see how things are progressing.

George You should have been a welfare worker, Aramis.

Aramis One has a flair—you know how it is. Cheers!

George Cheers!

They drink

Lights fade to Black-out

SCENE 2

The same. Late evening, a few days later

George is standing at the bar, polishing glasses with a tea-towel. DR *sit the Foreigners, their growing collection of brushes stacked about them. From the kitchen comes the sound of washing-up—wild, abandoned washing-up. George glances apprehensively in the direction of the clatter and sighs. There is a crash. He winces*

George (*calling through the arch*) Yvette, that's the fifth glass today. Why do you thrash about in the sink so?

Yvette (*off*) Oh, George, don't be cross. I've never used such a lovely big sink. It's such fun to swirl the water round. Whee!

George But it's very hard on the glassware.

Yvette (*off*) We can get some more. There! I won't do any more washing-up.

The sound of water running away

George Yvette, you must wash round the sink—otherwise it leaves a greasy scum.

Yvette (*off*) Ugh! I don't want to do that very much. Still just for once.

Yvette enters

George.

George Yes?

Yvette Am I a good housewife, eh? (*She embraces George*)

George Yes, of course, you will soon learn. Steady, Yvette! You are getting grease on my ears.

Yvette (*crossing* c) Oh, it's these silly nails. They're much too long for housework. I shall cut them off.

George (*following her*) No, no, Yvette! You have such lovely hands!

Yvette Two of them are broken already, George, see? It'll be a relief not to have to bother about them all the time.

George But you had such beautiful hands.

Yvette (*curling up on a chair* R *of the table* LC) It was my silly nails scratched the counter—and you didn't like that, did you?

George No, I didn't. But I explained, it takes a lot of work to keep the surface good.

Yvette I think that's nonsense. After all, it's our home. If one can't do damage in one's own home—I mean, it's not like those wretched furnished apartments where you're afraid of breaking something all the time.

George It's usual to take care of one's things, Yvette.

Yvette I didn't think a few casualties mattered—if they were your own.

George No, of course not. But please don't put us in the poorhouse. (*He shakes out a tea-towel*)

Yvette Oh, George!

George Now we have to wash the tea-towels.

Yvette I'm so tired. Let's do them tomorrow, George.

George But— all right little one, go to bed.

Yvette (*crossing to the bar*) Don't wake me when you come up. I shall be fast asleep in my curlers!

George Yvette! Do you have to sleep in curlers?

Yvette Why not? Then I can save my hairdressing money.

George What will you spend it on?

Yvette I'll—I'll pay for the glasses I broke.

George Yvette, my pet, you don't have to do that. This is a partnership. You can take it from the till.

Yvette I can go to the till?

George Well—yes—occasionally.

Yvette (*in wonder*) Oh! (*She leans over the counter*)

George (*anxiously*) Of course, Seraphine never takes very much. She is very careful with the money. She manages it all so well and——

Yvette (*not listening*) I can go to the till! (*She waggles her fingers*)

George takes Yvette's fingers, kisses them and places them firmly by her side

Good-night, George! (*She goes upstairs*)
George Good-night, Yvette. (*To himself*) Now, if I could just get those two out of the corner, I could sweep the floor. (*He begins clearing up*)

The Foreigners rise

Ah! You are leaving, sir?
Male Foreigner Mm. Er——
George Yes, yes, I will write it down as usual. Here!
Female Foreigner Lojim elif seriatij, voob! (*She pays*)

Male Foreigner loads up

Male Foreigner (*sighing*) Haag!
George Thank you. Wait, you have forgotten this! What a nice little ceiling brush!
Male Foreigner (*taking it unenthusiastically*) Mm. Goot-naat!
George Good-night! (*Calling*) If you stay here much longer you will speak the language like a native!

The Foreigners exit

Aramis passes the Foreigners on his way in

Aramis (*entering*) Hallo, George. (*Seeing the Foreigners*) Good gracious! Still here?
George They must have meant the car would take one month! Come in, Aramis. (*He goes behind the bar*)
Aramis What a collection of brushes!
George They'd bought two brooms and a besom before lunch and during the afternoon they acquired a hearthbrush, a carpet brush, a scrubbing brush and a clothes' whisk. A nightcap?
Aramis (*leaning on the bar*) How are things working out?
George Well, naturally it is all very strange to Yvette—but not too bad, you know. (*He pours a drink for Aramis*)
Aramis Good. I was sure it would be all right.
George Yes, yes, when she understands about things. Bless her, she was so happy this morning flapping about in a pair of Seraphine's old slippers. Do you know, Aramis, I never realized, but her ankles are not quite so slim as I always thought?
Aramis Well, what does that matter—if you have had a good day together.

George Frankly, it's been a rather tiring one and to tell the truth I'd give anything to turn in—but of course, there's Seraphine! I must say it will feel a bit peculiar.

Aramis (*chuckling*) Seraphine! Don't forget to spruce up, George.

George Of course not. I mustn't disappoint her. (*Yawning*) The walk will freshen me up.

Aramis What a lucky man.

George (*moving* C) Oh well, you know, I've you to thank really. I'd never have been able to think of this splendid—(*yawning*)—arrangement myself. I'll shut up now. No one seems to be about. (*He closes another shutter at the windows*)

Aramis How has Seraphine settled in?

George I don't know. I haven't heard. She was going to spend the day shopping, so as to be able to dress up for my benefit tonight.

Aramis How well she's co-operating.

George Yes, she's really getting into the spirit of the thing, bless her. (*He gets a tie from the pegs and moves* DL *to the mirror*)

Aramis I hope you've remembered a few little things for her.

George Oh yes! And I'm picking up some flowers on the way.

Aramis It's going to do her the world of good, George.

George I certainly hope so. (*Stifling another yawn*) I must pull myself together. Of course it had to be a busy day! (*Wandering to the bar and searching*) A little hair oil, I think. Now where? Ah, here we are. (*He finds the cruet bottles*)

Aramis (*sniffing*) No, no, George! What are you thinking of?

George Pure olive oil never harmed a hair of anyone's head, Aramis.

Aramis Very likely—but that's the vinegar.

George (*regarding the bottle with surprise*) Oh dear, dear.

Aramis Really, George, you must perk up.

George I'll have a drink.

Aramis I must be off, old friend. Best of luck.

George Thank you, Aramis.

Aramis goes out

George shuts the last shutter behind him, and makes for his drink. He is about to drink it when there is a knock

Oh there! Whoever is this? (*He opens the shutter*)

Seraphine enters. She is dressed in pretty pyjamas and négligé— covered by a coat

Seraphine!

Seraphine – tight-lipped – marches in to c *and unbuttoning her coat, casts it aside. George follows her* DC

Seraphine, what are you doing here? I mean, aren't I supposed to be coming to you? I mean, I was just getting ready to set out and——
Seraphine (*tragically*) The tank's burst!
George The tank!
Seraphine I could hear trickling water all the afternoon, but I didn't take any notice. And then all of a sudden the ceiling fell in!
George The ceiling!
Seraphine Right on to the divan.
George The divan!
Seraphine By the sheerest good chance I'd just got up from it.
George You're quite sure it's not just the damp?
Seraphine George! Ten gallons of cold water gushed down into that disgusting catacomb of a flat.
George (*anxiously*) You found the stopcock?
Seraphine Yes, I found the stopcock! And I mopped it up! And I rang the plumber! And I hung the bedclothes up! And our evening is completely ruined! (*She weeps across the bar*)
George (*hurrying to comfort her*) Oh, there, there, there, Seraphine, darling. Don't cry. I can't bear you to cry.
Seraphine Well, isn't it?
George No, no, no. It doesn't have to be. We can get over a little thing like a burst tank. Tch! That'll cost a pretty penny!
Seraphine How can we?
George Well, er—there must be a way. I mean, we could—er—I wish Aramis were here.
Seraphine Where am I going to sleep anyway?
George You must stay here of course.

He guides Seraphine towards the stairs, then, remembering Yvette, they halt

I'll get the camp bed out from the cupboard. (*He hurries to get it out, fighting off a broom or two*)
Seraphine (*tearfully*) It's no good, George.
George But of course it is. (*Dragging the bed to the centre and setting it up*) It's really not at all bad when you get it up.
Seraphine I mean the nice evening we planned.
George (*still coping*) A few cushions and things. You'll be as snug as a——
Seraphine We can't possibly have it now. And I got myself all ready! (*She removes the négligé to show off the pyjamas*)

George Look here, Seraphine, cheer up. This doesn't have to make any difference.

Seraphine But how?

George What does it matter where we are—as long as we're together. Mm?

Seraphine (*brightening*) You mean you'll stay here with me?

George Of course. We'll do as we said. I'll lock up!

Seraphine Oh, George, do you think we can? Turn the lights down and bring some more cushions.

George closes the shutter. Seraphine brings a mattress and rug from the cupboard.

George goes through the arch

The lights go down

George returns with cushions

George There!

Seraphine climbs over the bed and sits facing front

We'll be quite comfy. (*Sitting beside her rather awkwardly*) Let's turn in, my dear. (*He yawns*)

Seraphine Oh, no, George! That's not the way!

George But, Seraphine—it's getting late—and——

Seraphine George, you are not just going to slump into bed as usual. I insist on being treated as you treat Yvette. That was the arrangement. You know it was.

George Yes, I know, and I had it all planned but—well—I feel awkward.

Seraphine I don't. Come on, George, pull yourself together. Now go on out and I'll tell you when I'm ready.

George All right.

George goes out through the arch

Seraphine makes herself ready on the camp bed

While her back is turned, George dodges back on, gathers the flowers out of a vase on the bar and quickly exits again

Seraphine tries out a pose or two

Seraphine (*reclining seductively*) Ready, George.

George enters wearing a hat, carrying flowers and a box of chocolates

George Seraphine! (*He places the hat, flowers and chocolates on the bar and advances*)
Seraphine (*opening her arms*) Darling!
George (*lovingly*) Darling! Ah, my precious—my own—my—— (*changing his tone*) no, I can't—really, it's indecent!
Seraphine Nonsense! Give your mind to it.
George But I can't treat you like this—I—I respect you, Seraphine.
Seraphine I told you. Treat me as you do Yvette! Come—take me by storm!
George But I don't take Yvette by storm.
Seraphine Well, for heaven's sake, do whatever you do do!
George All right. I'll do my best.
Seraphine Go out and come in again. I've quite lost the train of thought.
George Very well, Seraphine. But remember I do this entirely to please you.
Seraphine Go, go, go! Your little Seraphine—your plaything, your comfort—awaits you! (*She sighs alluringly*)
George All right. I'll start again. Cheerio. But wait, if you really want to do the same as Yvette, she usually hides.
Seraphine Whatever for? Oh, I see, a little game.
George You don't have to.
Seraphine Oh yes! You go out and I'll hide.

George goes out

Seraphine moves round humming and chuckling. She peers into the cellar—thinks better of it. Opens the cupboard door—gets an armful of brooms for her pains; and finally she disappears under the bar

Ready!

George enters

George (*in cooing tones*) Seraphine! Seraphinette! Darling! Where are you? (*Peering about*) Where are you? What a clever little one you are!

He exits into the cellar—then after a moment re-emerges

(*Calling; a little edgily*) Seraphine! Where the—where are you? (*He opens the cupboard, replaces a clutch of brooms, and shuts it again and sucks in his breath impatiently*) I give up, dear! (*Pause, then yelling*) Seraphine!

Seraphine (*muffled*) Help! George! I'm stuck!

George Good gracious! Here, let me help. (*He heaves her out and brings her* D) You shouldn't squeeze into such a space. Remember your operation!

Seraphine Thank goodness! Well, what happens next? (*She sits on camp bed*)

George Oh yes—yes of course. (*Adopting a honeyed voice*) Here, sweetheart, a few flowers. (*He presents them*)

Seraphine Oh, darling, how sweet of you. You may embrace me!

George (*tersely*) No, no, not so fast! I just kiss your wrists— like this!

Seraphine (*approvingly*) Mm.

George And here—a few chocolates. (*He presents them*) To make my little pigeon plumper!

Seraphine (*in her own voice*) Plumper! You've always said you like me slim.

George Well, I do—but I like Yvette plump. Now, Seraphine, you want me to behave as I do with Yvette, don't you?

Seraphine (*cooing again*) Yes! Ah, you are too good to me, my darling, when I can give you so little in return.

George (*sitting on the bed, facing* U) But you give me everything, my treasure, you give me all the happiness I have in life. (*He breaks off hastily*) Er—that is—shall we sit by the fire and play Piquet?

Seraphine (*suggestively*) I'd much sooner just lie here and——

George Later, Seraphine, later! Aren't you going to give me a drink, my own?

Seraphine (*graciously*) Of course. Er—what do we have?

George I'll get it. Relax my dearest, lie back with your dark head against the red cushions and let me drink you in. How I wish I could see more of you.

Seraphine undoes her top button

Yes, indeed, I—no, no, Seraphine, not yet!

Seraphine (*a little impatiently*) All right.

George First we must celebrate! (*Darting across to the bar to find champagne and two glasses*) We must celebrate finding each other! Celebrate our happiness and the heaven we have created here in our cosy love nest. Your arms are my sweet retreat! You are my sanctuary. My heart bursts with love for you!

The champagne cork pops

Seraphine (*starting*) Oh!
George Champagne? (*He pours it*)
Seraphine Champagne? Oh, for a moment I thought——
George (*firmly*) Champagne, the best champagne! Nothing is too good
for you, my dove.
Seraphine I adore champagne—the best champagne!

They drink

George To you, my sweet! To your glorious eyes—your white throat—
your generous loving heart!

*During George's speech, Seraphine stretches herself full length, so
George sits on the floor* D

Seraphine As if I could refuse you anything when you speak to me like
that! Let me stroke your hair!
George (*sighing blissfully*) What have I done to deserve such exquisite
favours. Ah, Yvette—I mean, Seraphine, if only I were free—what a
life we would have!
Seraphine But you would never leave your wife!
George Never!
Seraphine I'm glad. I could never love a dishonourable man.
George What a treasure you are. You give me such a precious jewel—
your friendship! Whilst I can only offer the trivial recompense of a few
paltry emeralds. (*He produces a little jewel box and hands it to her*)
Seraphine (*squawking*) Emeralds!
George (*in a lower key*) Make room on the camp bed for me, my swan.
(*He turns* U *and starts clambering on*)
Seraphine Emeralds, is this usual? (*She kneels up*)
George Of course. Come my chicken! (*He kneels facing her*)
Seraphine (*in ominous tones*) How many of these did you give that
woman?
George Seraphine, please!—Do not break the mood!
Seraphine Emeralds—every time?
George No, no, of course not! Sometimes rubies. Darling Seraphine——
Seraphine Were did you get the money?
George Seraphine, you're ruining everything—you sound just like a
wife! Sweetheart!
Seraphine Don't sweetheart me. How many of these have you given
that hussy?

George Why, Seraphine! What is it? I have never heard you speak harshly of her before. You always said you didn't mind our relationship.

Seraphine I don't mind your relationship. I do mind emeralds. How could you afford such things?

George But, Seraphine, didn't I give you jewels on your birthday?

Seraphine Once a year—and you said it broke you!

George It did.

Seraphine Why?

George Because I'd just——(*Inspired*) Because they were real.

Seraphine You mean—these aren't?

George (*back-pedalling hard*) Now, would I buy such things for a mere friend—someone outside the family?

Seraphine That's right. And naturally a girl like Yvette wouldn't know the difference anyway.

George Of course not. Such a simple soul. It's quite touching how pleased she is with a little paste brooch now and again.

Seraphine (*sitting back on her haunches*) And you never give her valuable presents at all?

George Never! (*He sits back*)

Seraphine You're a hard man, George.

George I beg your pardon?

Seraphine No, no, George, one ought to be fair. Promise me you'll give her something worthwhile for Christmas.

George Yes, dear.

Seraphine No need to overdo it, mind. Now, where were we?

George (*with a stifled yawn*) I was nearly in the bed.

Seraphine (*interested*) Oh. Come on then.

With some difficulty they both get settled

There! Ah, George, lay your head here—no here—and let me caress you. Dear George, I've been waiting since lunchtime for you to come. George, I've been so excited. Did you like the outfit I bought? There was a sale at the store and I got nearly a third off. There's not a thing wrong with it, George. Do you like it?

George Um.

Seraphine (*eyes closed*) The plumber's coming in the morning. Maybe we could get some new curtains and covers—eh, George? Perhaps he'll look at the drains at the same time. (*She yawns*) I rather like this camp bed. It's quite... comfortable when you get used to it... Not so soft as our bed—but comfortable. I hope the canvas is strong enough... Oh, George, I'm feeling sleepy and I did so want to be a success... successful... tomorrow night, George... (*She sighs off to sleep*)

From George comes a gentle snore and soon there is a duet of peaceful sleepers

Fade to Black-out

ACT II

SCENE 1

The same. Morning, one week later

The camp bed is gone. George is once more behind the bar serving Aramis

George —but the unfair thing was, Aramis, that she was furious in the morning. And I can't say things have gone properly since.

Aramis (*sitting on a stool*) Well, naturally, old man. And there was I imagining things were all right.

George Not at all, I'm afraid. I hoped you'd come in today. Where have you been lately?

Aramis I'm very sorry. I had no intention of abandoning you. I'm very interested in the experiment for one thing. But I was clearing up at the office before going on leave.

George You're going away?

Aramis Just for a month or so.

George Oh.

Aramis Visiting a friend in Boulogne.

George (*miserably*) How nice.

Aramis (*airily*) And of course I shall take a trip or two over to Dover. Just to brush up my English. You know—and to see a stamp dealer who usually has something for me.

George (*enviously*) Ah, what it is to travel!

Aramis But of course, George, we must get you straightened out first.

George Frankly, Aramis, I don't think either Seraphine or Yvette have found things as they expected. Especially Seraphine. Although she's brazening it out, I wouldn't be surprised if she wanted to change back again.

Aramis So soon? Why she hasn't given it a fair trial.

George (*bitterly*) It's been a fair trial for me, I assure you!

Aramis Are you doing your best, George?

George Best! Aramis, I am absolutely worn out! what with doing all the domestic jobs that Yvette forgets and keeping the books in order. And Seraphine! She was never jealous of Yvette before!

Aramis It strikes me, George, you've rather mishandled this situation. I'm afraid the fact has to be faced that you just don't understand women.

George But I am trying my best to please them both! I love them. Aramis. What can I do?

Aramis Now, now, don't upset yourself. Just let me think. I believe I'll go and call on Seraphine—if you've no objection.

George No, no! Oh, Aramis—take these tomatoes to her. She asked me to get them. It's awkward for her not going out you know—but since she's supposed to have gone away...

Aramis I'll give them to her. Goodbye, George. (*Starting to leave*) Mm. No one in the corner today? Pierre must have mended their car at last.

George He must have. What a relief!

The Foreigners enter U, *carrying their load of brooms and brushes*

Male Foreigner Goot morn!
George Dear lord!
Aramis (*going*) Old Pierre must be planning to retire!

Aramis exits

The foreign couple make themselves comfortable as best they can with their load, at the table LC *She sits* L *He sits behind it*

George (*calling through the arch*) Coffee please, Yvette! For two! (*He watches through the arch for a moment*) No, no, no—those cups.

George exits into the kitchen

Male Foreigner (*resignedly*) So, abit anket dagen!
Female Foreigner (*accusingly*) In seg ye intoinepecticum muss!
Male Foreigner Nah, nah, nah! Es rotofarm kapus.
Female Foreigner Huh! So sihn dens!

George and Yvette enter. George carrying the coffee

George Bring the sugar, Yvette.
Yvette Where is it?
George I think there is some under the counter! (*To the Foreigners*) There! Two nice hot coffees!

Yvette passes George the sugar and he sets it on the table

Female Foreigner Pliz, dihn carfee teefestock es.
George Er—I beg your pardon?

Yvette moves C; *giggling*

Male Foreigner Dihn carfee—teefestook! Teefestook!
George Too hot? Too—you know—sip—ouch!—hot?
Female Foreigner Mussee vazz!

Yvette bursts out laughing

George Yvette, please! I'm sorry, madam, I don't understand.
Male Foreigner Teefestook! Mussee vazz!
Female Foreigner Mussee vazz! Teefestook!

Yvette collapses with mirth

George Yes, yes, sir, certainly! (*Aside*; *to Yvette*) Yvette, control
  yourself! One treats customers with respect!
Yvette They sound like a couple of soda syphons!
George Even so—one still keeps one's dignity.
Female Foreigner (*to Male Foreigner*) Voob, forgitzi es.

*They shrug, smile pathetically at George and turn their attention to their
coffee*

George Heavens know what they want. I only hope it's nothing
  important. Yvette, stop giggling please. Try to remember we have a
  business to run here. A duty to give the best service we can.

  Raymond approaches

Yvette I'm sorry, George.
George Now, here comes the Perrot fellow. Off to the kitchen, Yvette.
  (*He goes behind the bar*)
Yvette Why? I'd like to stop and help you serve.
George No, no, no.
Yvette You always send me out when he comes in.
George Not at all. Stay by all means if you wish to. But I'd rather you
  didn't. I leave it to you.
Yvette Very well. I shall stay. Good morning! (*She kneels on a chair* R
  facing upstage)

Raymond enters and greets George, eyeing Yvette with interest

Raymond Just a quick one, George. We lost last night.
George Too bad—never mind—there is always tonight. You can't win all the time. After all, last time they——
Raymond (*to Yvette*) Well! Who are you then, eh? George, who is this then? George!
George May I introduce my—er—cousin—Yvette.
Raymond (*admiringly*) How do you do. (*He shakes Yvette's hand*)

Yvette turns and sits

Raymond Well! Enchanting. So you're George's cousin, eh? Lucky for you there's no family likeness. (*He sits* R *of the table*)

George laughs uneasily

Raymond Staying for long, Yvette?
George Just until Seraphine gets back. She's taking a little trip.
Raymond (*leaning close to Yvette*) George's cousin, eh? Where's George been hiding you all these years, Yvette?
Yvette In the Place Nap——
George (*hastily*) Yvette!
Raymond Have a drink with us, Yvette?
George No, no, no.
Yvette But I'd like one, George.
Raymond Of course she would. Don't be a killjoy, George.
George Well, just one. (*He pours it*)
Raymond Is he as strict with you all the time, Yvette?
Yvette No, not all the time.
Raymond Does he let you out in the evenings? Has anyone shown you the delights of the town, Yvette? Mm? What about it, Yvette? Can you get out some night for a stroll?
Yvette Well——
George No!
Raymond What a spoilsport. Just because you're her uncle
George I did not say uncle, I said cousin.
Raymond What's the difference. You shouldn't keep her on a chain. (*Taking a chair from* L, *pulling it nearer Yvette and sitting astride it, regarding her admiringly*) Do you know... Yes! We've met before. (*He smiles sweetly at Yvette*)
George You have not!
Raymond Yes we have. Just a minute and I'll think where. (*He ponders*)
George (*to Yvette*) Have you?

Yvette shrugs, rises and leans across bar, smiling at Raymond. George is in torment

Raymond No, I think it's just that you remind me of someone else. That girl who lives in the Place—you know the one I mean. You know—that girl who lives in the Place—the Place—Place de Gaulle.
George (*greatly relieved*) Ah well, Yvette doesn't live anywhere near there. And I'm afraid she is not likely to be coming out in the evenings. She is doing the books with me.
Raymond Ah ha.
George Yes. Seraphine asked us to enter up a new ledger for her.
Yvette Uh?
George Don't worry, Yvette, I'll show you how. Meantime run along and make the beds. (*He pushes Yvette upstairs*)
Yvette (*going*) I have made it!

Yvette exits upstairs

George winces

Raymond What a nice little cousin, George. Everyone should have a nice little cousin like that up his sleeve. Now, if I had a nice little——
George Off to work now! Drink up, Raymond.
Raymond Yes, yes. (*Indicating the Foreigners*) Those two are still with us then?
George Yes, indeed. Every day they wander in. Poor souls. I should have thought they'd have gone on to Spain by train.
Raymond Spain—rubbish. They're a couple of Peruvians on a world tour. Won it in a TV contest. They told me.
George On your way, Raymond.

George guides Raymond to the door. Halfway there Raymond calls upstairs

Raymond (*calling*) Goodbye, Yvette! Pooh! No more a distant cousin of George's than I am! Less, come to think of it—because my old aunt's stepfather married George's great-grandfather——
George Come on! Come on! (*He drags Raymond out*)
Raymond (*pausing at the door to blow a kiss to the Foreigners*) All my love!

Raymond exits with George

Yvette comes downstairs and stands leaning on the bar

George enters with two glasses which he places on the bar

George Now, Yvette, I am just going down the road to meet Aramis. You can take charge for a little while. How would you like that?
Yvette But——
George All you have to do is ask what they want and give it to them.
Yvette That sounds easy enough.
George I'll be back in a few minutes. (*He removes his apron and heads for the door*)

The Foreigners jump up and waylay him

Male Foreigner Pliz, uns wutzi ap stiebelhumfin.
George Eh?

Yvette curls up with silent laughter

Female Foreigner Stiebelhumfin! Sh! Sh! Sh! Sh! Wooooo!

Female Foreigner gives a good imitation of a train. Male Foreigner joins her and they travel in a little circle together for George's benefit

George Ah, a train! The station! Yes, yes! I will show you the way. Come along. (*He heads towards the door*)

The Foreigners gather their belongings and follow George to the door

Not very frequent!
Male Foreigner Uh?
George Not many choo! choo!

George "steams" out U, followed by the Foreigners

Yvette, giggling, goes and stands at the door to watch them go. She then returns downstage. She sighs. She flicks at the bar with a duster, then abandons it and wanders off upstairs

Aunt Marie appears U. She is elderly, dressed in sober clothes and carrying a small suitcase. She approaches the café, enters, looks around and finding no one about, exits into the kitchen. She immediately reappears and crosses to the cellar door. She opens it, peers in, then withdraws with a frustrated grunt. She moves to the cupboard door, opens it, and receives a cascade of brooms. Very irritated now, she replaces the brooms and closes the cupboard door. She then crosses and goes upstairs

George and Aramis approach outside, talking as they enter the café

George Yes, yes and so…?

Aramis I just explained it away by saying I happened to be passing.

George She was delighted to see you, of course.

Aramis I think so. I began very cautiously, telling her how everyone was missing her.

George Of course.

Aramis She seemed rather concerned about the state of the accounts. Oh, and she asked me to remind you to collect the sheets from the laundry on Friday. She says it throws everyone out if you don't.

George Yes, yes, yes, but how is she getting on herself? I mean, what are her feelings now?

Aramis Well, George, as a matter of fact I've had a superb notion.

George No! What a man!

Aramis Quite obviously Seraphine is pining to return to the café. She's quite sure there will be a financial crisis if she doesn't.

George (*wryly*) What a shrewd women.

Aramis And that you will neglect all sorts of obvious duties — such as feeding the hens——

George Feeding the—great heavens! The hens! Excuse me a moment.

Aramis Wait! Another second won't make any difference. Now the point is, you say Yvette is quite happy still?

George She seems to be.

Aramis Well, you must begin acting more like a husband and put an end to all that.

George But——

Aramis Expect her to behave like Seraphine.

George But, Aramis—she's not used to——

Aramis Start complaining when little things go wrong.

George But that wouldn't be fair.

Aramis George, you want everyone to be contented again, don't you? Well, I've no doubt Seraphine will be much more resigned to her lot when she gets back here. It's just up to you to convince Yvette that she is better off in Place Napoleon.

George (*moving to the bar*) I see your point, Aramis. Tch! Now look at these dirty things. I'll start right away. Yvette! Where is she? You see, I leave her in charge for five minutes and she just disappears. What if there had been a customer!

Aramis Well, there's no one here. (*He moves* DL)

George They probably went away. Yvette!
Aramis Maybe she's out at the back—feeding the hens.
George She doesn't even know we keep hens! And we probably don't now! Excuse me!

Yvette comes downstairs

Oh, Yvette—there you are!
Yvette What's the matter?
George Where were you? You mustn't leave the place unattended like that! After all the till——
Yvette (*moving* DC) I was upstairs with your aunt.
George (*coming* D *between Aramis and Yvette*) Well, you mustn't go running upstairs with my aunt. You must understand——(*It sinks in*) My aunt!
Yvette Yes. Your Aunt Marie—from Dijon.
Aramis Oh dear!
George (*astounded*) Aunt Marie! But what is she doing here?
Yvette She said you telephoned saying I was coming to Dijon and then no one arrived so she got interested and decided to——
George Oh, good heavens, I forgot to call back cancelling the arrangement!
Aramis But saying "You" were coming Yvette. Surely it was Seraphine who was going to Dijon.
Yvette Well, yes—but I mean that's who she thinks I am.
George What!
Yvette Well, what was I supposed to do? You weren't here and she walked in and came straight up and kissed me and called me Seraphine and I didn't know how to explain who I was or what I was doing here.
George I can understand that.
Yvette So I said nothing—and now she's upstairs unpacking.
George }
Aramis } (*together*) Unpacking!
George Well, here's a nice thing.
Aramis (*consulting his watch*) My! The time is getting on. I have to meet—

Aramis starts off but George catches him

George (*frantically*) Aramis, don't leave me! What am I to do?
Aramis Calm down, George. Your aunt won't stay for ever. You just have to bluff it out.

George (*groaning*) She has never visited us before. Never! And now she comes! What an unreasonable woman.

Yvette I think I'd like to go back to Place Napoleon!

George A few moments ago that would have been splendid, but now it's too late.

Yvette Why don't you just tell her the truth?

George How can I do that! I hardly know her. And it's not the sort of thing you just blurt out to someone the moment they step over your threshold—especially if it's your sole-surviving, elderly, rather wealthy maiden aunt.

Yvette No, I suppose not.

Aunt Marie comes downstairs, still wearing her hat

Aunt Marie Ah! George!

George Aunt Marie!

Aunt Marie George dear—after all these years—and you haven't changed a bit!

George Oh, now Auntie, I must have aged. I certainly feel as if I have.

Aunt Marie Not a bit of it. Dear George! (*She hugs and kisses George on both cheeks*)

George May I present my friend, Aramis.

Aramis Madam! (*He bows over Aunt Marie's hand*)

George I'm sorry about the message Auntie, there was a mix-up.

Yvette makes herself scarce DR

Aunt Marie I should think there was. Naturally, I started preparing to receive Seraphine, then when you didn't arrive, my dear, I thought perhaps something was wrong. But then, I reasoned, bad news usually travels faster than good and surely they would let me know. So at last I got so curious, I just threw a few things in a bag and jumped on a train and came here.

George Well, as you see, everything is all right.

Aunt Marie (*moving* C) I'm so relieved, but really it was a good excuse to come and visit you at last—and meet dear Seraphine. Fancy all this time and never a glimpse of you, Seraphine. Ah, you young people who run off and get married and cheat your relations of a jolly wedding! Well, never mind, so long as you've been happy. And you have, of course, Seraphine?

No answer

Seraphine?

George Yvette, Auntie's talking to you!
Yvette (*crossing to Aunt Marie*) Oh! Yes, yes, of course! (*Aside; to George*) Did you really elope?
Aunt Marie "Yvette"? Why do you call her Yvette?
Aramis It's short for Seraphine, Madam—in these parts.
Aunt Marie How curious. Well, I shall call you Seraphine. I don't like abbreviations. (*Sitting* R *of the table* LC) Sit down, my dears.

George, Yvette and Aramis sit

Well, now at last I shall have the opportunity to get to know you properly, Seraphine. I must say George, this is a very pleasant place. I shall just enjoy a nice long stay here with you both. (*She removes her hat and settles back*)

The others slowly rise in dismay

Fade to Black-out

SCENE 2

The same. Midday, two weeks later

The table LC *is laid with cutlery and cruet*

Aunt Marie is sitting outside the café, examining a chair cover. She rises and enters, carrying the cover. She peers through the arch into the kitchen where a clatter of pots is heard.

Aunt Marie (*calling*) Seraphine! Ah, there you are. Getting lunch already? My word, what an interesting smell. Seraphine, dear, would you just slip upstairs for my spectacles, I'm afraid I can't mend this chair cover for you without them.
Yvette (*off*) But, George told you Aunt Marie, it really isn't necessary.
Aunt Marie Nonsense, Seraphine, I like to make myself useful.
Yvette (*off*) Oh, very well.

Yvette enters

I just didn't want to leave that pot.
Aunt Marie A stitch in time saves nine, you know.
Yvette Where are the spectacles?
Aunt Marie On the chest in my room—you can't miss them.

Yvette runs upstairs

(*Calling*) Oh, Seraphine, we'll need some green thread too. Have you some?

Yvette (*off; in the distance*) Green thread? I don't know!

Aunt Marie You can't mend it without. At least—what colours have you got?

Yvette (*off; still distant*) I—I don't know. They're not on the chest.

Aunt Marie Try the little bag on my——

There is a hiss from the kitchen

Oh, Seraphine! Something's boiling over, dear!

Yvette hurries downstairs

You left it on too great a heat didn't you?

Yvette Yes. Oh dear!

Yvette crosses to kitchen and goes in

Aunt Marie (*peering in*) Never mind. I'll wipe it up for you. Where's the cloth?

Yvette (*off*) Out there on the counter.

Aunt Marie (*finding the cloth and examining it disapprovingly*) Oh. This could do with a scalding, don't you think?

Yvette (*off*) Yes, I expect so.

Aunt Marie I'll do it later when the kitchen's a little clearer! It's wonderful how you can work in such a muddle. And where's the sewing basket? Ah, I can see it myself. (*She produces it from underneath the bar*)

Yvette (*off*) Thank goodness!

Aunt Marie Well, now—mm—we don't seem to have green. There's brown here—do you think that will do?

Yvette looks out from the kitchen

Yvette What?

Aunt Marie Brown?

Yvette Yes, use brown.

Yvette goes back into the kitchen

Aunt Marie Brown! Well, each to his own taste, I suppose. Still, I don't think it will look very nice, Seraphine!

Yvette (*off*) Well, leave it then.

Aunt Marie I expect they'd have some green thread across at the store.
Yvette (*off*) But I'm in the middle of——
Aunt Marie All right, all right, dear, I'll go.
Yvette (*off*) Oh, thank you.
Aunt Marie Now, where did I put my coat? Seraphine!
Yvette (*off*) I don't know!
Aunt Marie There! It must be up in my room.
Yvette (*off*) Oh.

Yvette enters

All right. I'll go. (*She starts out*)
Aunt Marie That's all right, dear. I'll go.
Yvette Good!

Yvette goes back into the kitchen

Aunt Marie Don't forget to salt those vegetables, Seraphine.
Yvette (*off*) I have salted them.
Aunt Marie I don't think so, dear.
Yvette (*off*) I tell you——
Aunt Marie But I'm sure! You taste it, Seraphine. (*She starts to go upstairs*)
Yvette (*off*) Oh, very well—but I'm absolutely certain——(*She screams*) Oh, I've burnt my lip!

Yvette runs out to c

Aunt Marie (*coming* D) Oh gracious! Quickly—put some butter on it.
Yvette Oh, go away! (*She sits* R *of the table, holding her mouth*)
Aunt Marie No, no, Seraphine! Let me look at it. (*She does so*) Dear, dear. I think you'll get a blister. Sit down dear, I'll finish off the lunch.
Yvette I can manage!
Aunt Marie No, no, no.

Aunt Marie goes into the kitchen, then pops her head back

You really should have wiped this stove, dear. It's so much more difficult to clean when it's burnt on hard, Seraphine.

Aunt Marie disappears into the kitchen and is heard in the distance humming and clattering

Yvette (*to herself*) If she calls me Seraphine again, I shall throw a pot at her!

George enters from the cellar carrying bottles

Yvette George! Oh, George! (*She runs up to him*)
George Whatever is the matter?
Yvette Oh, George, she's driving me mad!
George Why, what's she doing?
Yvette She's pestering and interfering and questioning and criticizing and watching and timing and—oh, George, I'm doing everything wrong!
George There, there, there! You wanted to be a proper wife, Yvette. All wives have their husband's relations come and do that sort of thing.
Yvette I never knew!
George Yes, well, you're learning—aren't you? (*He crosses to the bar*)
Yvette It's horrid. She says I do everything the wrong way.
George (*placing the bottles*) Well, it's a lot worse for you, of course, because you probably do.
Yvette Well, I tell you, I can't stand any more of it.
George Sh! Sh! For heaven's sake, Yvette! There are customers coming in.

The Foreigners appear upstage

Yvette Those two! They don't understand a thing. (*She moves* DL)
George They can hear the tone of your voice, can't they? That's the same in any language, I presume! Anyway, they are learning more every day. (*Calling to the Foreigners*) Good-day to you!
The Foreigners (*entering*) Good da. Iv yo pliz, warn.

George moves towards the Foreigners

George Splendid, sir! Spoken like a Frenchman! You see, Yvette? Here you are, sir! (*He guides them* DR) And what have we bought today? Mm, a little lint chaser. Very useful!
Female Foreigner (*sitting*) Eberwib ged mudder brutzi ig gos maad!
Male Foreigner (*sitting*) Tch! Tch!
George Now Yvette – back to the kitchen, please. We cannot continue this conversation in the café. (*He pours wine*)
Yvette (*going behind the bar*) Well, hurry up and close for lunch. I've had enough of Aunt Marie on my own.
George It's not time yet! Never mind, as soon as these two go we will eat anyway.
Yvette We'd better!
George But don't forget we must wait for Aramis.

Yvette (*glancing upstage*) He is coming across the square now.

George What? So he is. Thank goodness. Run along now, Yvette, my little one, or the meal will be spoiled.

Yvette (*moving to the arch*) With Aunt Marie supervising? How could it be!

Yvette exits into the kitchen

George sighs and crosses to serve the two Foreigners

Aramis enters, carrying a suitcase

When he thinks of it, George lays plates and glasses on the table during the following conversation

Aramis (*approaching George*) Hallo, old friend. How goes it?

George Need you ask? (*In horror*) Aramis, why the suitcase?

Aramis My leave, George I start today. I told you. I leave for Boulogne on the two-thirty. (*He sits* U *of the table* LC)

George What shall I do?

Aramis Isn't your aunt supposed to go tomorrow?

George I'm keeping my fingers crossed! But I'll be lost without you, Aramis!

Aramis It can't be helped, old friend. Anyway, I've come to lunch again as you asked me. I trust I do not wear out my welcome.

George Oh, Aramis, if you only knew what a godsend it has been having you eat with us. You are so adept at keeping the conversation on general lines. When we are all three on our own, Aunt Marie plunges into family matters which get Yvette quite out of her depth. Believe me, breakfast is a nightmare!

Aramis I would have made breakfast if I could, George, but you rise so early.

George Yes, yes, I understand, and anyway Aunt Marie might have thought it peculiar.

Aramis How is Yvette impressing your aunt?

George How could she? Aunt Marie thinks her a complete fool about the house—and of course she is! Any minute the whole business may be exposed.

Aramis Oh come! There is many a housewife blissfully stirring a ruined sauce at this very moment. Don't we know some splendid incompetents in this very town?

George One who doesn't know where she keeps her own casseroles? Aunt Marie is not so simple, believe me. Already I have detected a gleam of suspicion in her eye. I'm sure I have. Oh, Aramis, surely she won't stay much longer!

Aramis Ah, George, there's nothing so enjoyable to a woman as disorganizing another woman's home.

George So it seems.

Aramis Never fear, George. Her memories of Saladup will be so pleasant, she'll remember you all the more generously.

George Do you think so?

Aramis Whereas if Seraphine had been here, running things faultlessly, your aunt would have departed in a fury of frustration and cut you out of her will altogether.

George I suppose it's possible.

Aramis Depend on it, George. I know them, dear fellow. I know them!

George How is Seraphine? Although I hardly dare ask.

Aramis Yes, well, the news is not too good, George. May I be blunt?

George You'd better. I'm sure she was.

Aramis She was. She's finished with Place Napoleon, George.

George But what is she—where is she——? Aramis, she can't come here!

Aramis So I told her, George, but she declared she would rather spend the rest of her life in Tut-ankh-amen's tomb than another night in——

George Why is she so fanciful!

Aramis I did my best to stall her off, George. But she was determined to leave.

George She's coming here?

Aramis Where else, George? Short of coming to me and naturally that was out of the question.

George (*desperately*) Why?

Aramis My dear fellow! For obvious reasons! Anyway I have only the narrowest of single beds—a mere clothes-line.

George (*wildly*) What about the sofa? You have a sofa! Oh yes you have. You have a sofa. I've seen it. A sofa! *A sofa!*

Aramis George! Control yourself! It's away having its springs set up.

George How disgusting! (*Clutcing Aramis*) And why this week? Eh? Why not last week—or next week? Why? *Why?*

Aramis George, please! Let go of my lapels!

George (*sitting* R *of the table* LC; *weakly*) I'm sorry, Aramis, but it's getting beyond me. If Seraphine turns up—everything will come out. When is she likely to arrive?

Aramis I left her packing.

George groans and gropes for Aramis' hand

Now don't weaken, George. (*Grasping George's hand firmly*) I'm here
for a little longer and we'll deal with the situation when it arises.
George You're a tower of strength, Aramis!

Yvette appears in the arch

Yvette Lunch is ready, George.
Aramis Ah!
George Where is Aunt Marie?
Yvette Whipping the cream. She would whip it.
George Oh dear, dear. Let's get it in.
Aramis I'll help you.

George, Yvette and Aramis exit through the arch

Female Foreigner (*moaning*) Ig kend wib neder naben kamt! Was
idossi! Kamtin ens so eldes caren!
Male Foreigner Es bondet caren isit.
Female Foreigner Al yaren modza follint es! (*Quoting sarcastically*)
Gese ant France, voob! Gesee ant France, voob!
Male Foreigner Oh! Do, es al maren modza follint uh?
Female Foreigner Vis neder kampt als yaren modza aljehuberhite!
Male Foreigner Neever maren modza oss!
Female Foreigner Wooser ens coolt! Alen zat lender nazin inpolkein!
Male Foreigner Lender nazin! Lender nazin! Ket gint uns yaren
modza!
Female Foreigner Maren modza!
Male Foreigner Yaren modza. Ans hiren vader win grosvacatzin
neder!
Female Foreigner (*furiously*) Vacatzin! Wadder vacatzin win haft!
Male Foreigner (*exasperatedly*) Oh bleisshofft!

*George, Aramis and Yvette enter, George and Aramis are carrying a
casserole and plates which they place on the table*

The Foreigners lapse into a strained silence

Aramis You are leaving the couple in the corner?
George Yes. They will go for a walk soon. Every afternoon it is the
same. I'll shut up then.

Aunt Marie enters

They all settle at the table LC. *Aramis* UL, *Yvette* DR, *Aunt Marie* DL,
George UR, *bringing himself a stool*

Aramis (*shaking Aunt Marie's hand*) Good-day to you, madam.
Aunt Marie Well, you eat with us again, sir. What a pleasure!
Aramis You honour me, madam.

Yvette removes the lid of the casserole. All blanche. Yvette serves

George Yvette—give Aunt Marie a larger helping.
Aunt Marie (*regarding her plate with disapproval*) No thank you.
  George, what did you do with the collection of recipes of your dear
  mother?
George They are here, Auntie, we use them all the time.
Aunt Marie Not all the time you don't.
George Well, today Yvette thought she would try it in the Greek style.
Aunt Marie But it is a dish of Provence——
Aramis No, no, madam, they have it in Greece also, I assure you.
  A favourite of a king, I understand. Have I ever shown you my
  unperforated three drachmas?
Aunt Marie I beg your pardon?
Aramis Picked them up quite by chance in a little shop in Marseilles.
Aunt Marie Marseilles. Ah! I bet that brings back memories,
  Seraphine?
Yvette (*uneasily*) Er—memories?
Aunt Marie How I smiled when I received that postcard from George.
  What did it say now? "No more need for a hot-water bottle!"

Uneasily, George moves to the bar for a bottle of wine

Yvette Yes, well, the—the weather changed I suppose.
Aunt Marie The weather changed! Isn't she quaint. It was your
  honeymoon—don't you remember?
Yvette Yes, of course! I was joking. Ha ha ha! (*Aside; to George*) A
  honeymoon in Marseilles?
George (*quickly*) We stayed with Uncle Juvier.
Aunt Marie Seraphine knows that, George.
George (*sitting*) I was telling Aramis.
Aunt Marie Oh yes. Mm. (*She looks hard at George and Yvette, then
  goes on pecking at her food*)
George Wine?
Yvette (*fervently*) Yes, please!
Aunt Marie Wine for you, my dear? But I understood you could not
  drink it?
George Just a little on special occasions. Such as your visit, Aunt
  Marie.

Aunt Marie But, my dear, you must be careful. George, I don't think you should allow her——
Yvette George, if you don't pour me a glass——!
George Yes, yes, Yvette! Really, Auntie, it's perfectly all right.
Aunt Marie Oh. Your little trouble has cleared up then, Seraphine?
Yvette (*decidedly*) Yes.
Aunt Marie I'm so glad. Well, perhaps now we may hope for some interesting news in the future?
Yvette (*recklessly*) Why not?
George (*warningly*) Yvette!
Aunt Marie (*archly*) Ah, ha ha! I saw that look between you. You don't mean you and George have a little secret?
George No, no, no, no! Aramis, tell us some more about the Baden Neun Kreuzer Green. This is fascinating, Aunt Marie.
Aunt Marie (*softly*; *to Yvette*) I understand. Not in front of strangers, eh? You must tell me all about it after he's gone, dear.

George groans

Aramis The unusual thing was in the colour, you see. Now these particular stamps should have had a pale mauve background, but by some strange mischance one set were printed on green paper. Imagine! And the odd thing was. . . .

The Foreigners rise, collect their pile of brushes and brooms and start out

Male Foreigner Pliz, moga veegum ma bin hosfelete.
George Oh?
Female Foreigner Sirt hosfele es doorsist.
George Well, yes, yes. Aramis!

Aramis rises and moves c

Aramis Beg pardon, madam, what was that again?
Male Foreigner Hosfelete 1 beida hosfelete! (*He waves his hand in the air*)
Aunt Marie What are they talking about, George?
George I only wish I knew, Auntie.
Male Foreigner Med wodus comeket. Niss indoorsit noodalongitmoga evegum hesinegor hosfelete!
Male Foreigner ⎱
Female Foreigner ⎰ (*together*) Hesingor hosfelete.

The Foreigners both wave their hands

Aramis George! I do believe they're going!

George Going?—You mean for good? Of course! That's what they mean!

Aramis Well! Goodbye, sir and madam. So glad you're on your way at last!

George Yvette, say goodbye!

Yvette (*shaking hands with the Foreigners*) Goodbye—have a nice holiday.

George Auntie, these poor folk have been waiting so long for their car to be repaired and now at last they're off again!

Aunt Marie (*shaking hands with the Foreigners*) Never mind, I'm sure you enjoyed your stay in Saladup. Such a pretty place, don't you think?

Male Foreigner Uh?

George (*shaking hands with the Foreigners*) Goodbye, my dear sir—madam! We did enjoy having you! I trust you'll have no more trouble on your journey! Farewell!

Everyone waves enthusiastically to the bewildered Foreigners who walk out of the door and settle in the chairs outside the café. Pause

That was not what they meant, Aramis.

They all throw up their hands and resume the meal

Aramis And as I was saying, the odd thing was that it wasn't discovered until nearly fifty years after——

George Everyone finished? There's a lot left.

Yvette George, will you bring the tomatoes?

George Yes, of course. (*Taking the casserole from Yvette*) Had enough, Aunt Marie?

Aunt Marie More than enough, thank you.

George exits through the arch into the kitchen, with the casserole

Aramis Yes, fifty years after — by which time, of course, most of them had been destroyed as you can imagine. But there are still existing three of these rarities and of course they are worth considerable ——

Raymond approaches u

Raymond (*singing*) With a roll on the drum here they come, here they come!

Raymond enters the café and makes for the bar. He is slightly drunker than usual and waving a newspaper triumphantly. There is a general greeting

George enters with a plate of tomatoes. He sees Raymond and freezes. Then he places the plate on the table

An early lunch today, eh? Mm. Yum yum. Very nice smell.

George Yes, yes. Good-morning, Raymond. As usual? (*Going behind the bar and serving Raymond; calling back to Aramis, loudly*) Do carry on, Aramis!

Aramis (*continuing the same*) There is something I would like to tell you about a strange Faroe Island. (*Leaning across to Aunt Marie*) I don't know if you ever heard about it? (*He takes a quick mouthful of food*)

Raymond Now, here's the proof, George! (*Flourishing the newspaper*) Look here, you see, a photograph. Proof!

George Well——

Raymond }
Aramis } (*together*) It's all in the position of the head.

Raymond and Aramis stop and look across at each other

Raymond Did you ever see a photo of Alfred Goullet? Did you? There was a man! Crouched down over the bars.

Aramis Sometimes one gets them upside down——

Raymond Concentrating straight ahead——

Aramis Sometimes a little to the right or left.

Raymond But the things about this fellow is—he's young. Young, George! I tell you he rides like an angel!

Aramis But sideways! Can you imagine that?

George Oh, he's got the speed, I grant you. If he could only control the wobble.

Raymond Ah, the wobble!

Aramis The back of the head leaning on the base and the profile pointing upwards.

George (*pointing at the newspaper*) You can almost see it here.

Raymond That is a blur, George, not a wobble—how can you see a wobble? All right all right, but look at the man himself! What do you see, mm?

Aramis Of course, not in the best condition.

Raymond In tip top condition!

Aramis and Raymond regard each other quite crossly

Aunt Marie Excuse me, would you pass the salt, Seraphine.
Yvette Oh, yes—here Aunt. (*She does so*)
Raymond (*glancing round; puzzled*) Seraphine?

George throws his arm round Raymond and guides his attention back on the newspaper. He pours Raymond another large drink

Aramis (*moving his chair yet nearer to Aunt Marie*) I have four Mauritius overprints you might like to hear about, madame. I got hold of them in a rather unusual way. I happened to be staying in Avignon in a little house in the wall, and the child of the house had a stamp collection. Just a child's set, of course, but among them I found these exceptional ones. How they came to be there he couldn't explain, but his uncle was seafaring and I fancy must have picked them up on his travels and given them to the boy.
Aunt Marie George, aren't you ever going to eat your tomato?
George Coming, Auntie! (*To Raymond*) Here, take the bottle, old man. Sit out in the sun with the newspaper.

George pushes Raymond towards the door, but Raymond resists and stays by the bar. He is sagging slightly now

Raymond Thanks, George. Here's to — here's to your — little cousin. (*He waves his glass and winks towards Yvette*)
Aunt Marie (*thinking the wink is for her*) Cousin?
George (*diving to the table*) Aunt, Aunt, Aunt! (*Sitting*) Aren't these delicious! My word what fragrance! (*To Yvette*) You certainly made a good job of these, my dear.
Yvette (*crossly*) Your aunt did them!
George Oh well. Very nice. Very nice, eh Aramis?
Aramis (*ploughing on doggedly*) One of my stamps was discovered in a very curious way. Stuck over a light leak in an old camera. It happened this way.

Aramis and George glance at Raymond who is immersed in his newspaper again

Raymond (*mumbling*) All that talk about legs and shoulders——
Aramis One day they had a tremendous spring clean and out went the camera into the dustbin——
Raymond It's heart a rider needs. It's here inside——
Aramis As I passed the dustbins I chanced to knocked against it——
Raymond I say the cycle was jostled——

Aramis Knocked against it——
Raymond Jostled! So who by? Who by?
Aramis I jostled the cycle and out fell the dustbin. I mean the camera—
—(*he mops his brow*)
Aunt Marie I'm not at all sure I follow you, Mr Aramis.
Yvette I'll fetch the pudding. (*She collects the plates*)
Aunt Marie No, Seraphine, I'll get it. I know where I put the cream.

Raymond stares at them again, frowning

Yvette (*sitting*) All right, then. If you're sure.

Aunt Marie takes the plates and crosses to the bar

Aunt Marie I can manage perfectly well, Seraphine.

Aunt Marie exits into the kitchen

Raymond looks at George who leaps up to the bar

Raymond What did she call her?
George Nothing, nothing!
Aramis (*joining them*) What do you think of Lemaitre's chances then, Raymond?
Raymond Who? Huh! Couldn't win against a bathchair.
George No, no, he has possibilities.
Aramis I believe there is an article about him. Why don't you read it outside?
George Yes, why don't you come outside, Raymond.

George and Aramis move encouragingly ∪

Aunt Marie appears from the kitchen with a large flan

Raymond moves tipsily towards Aunt Marie

Raymond Permit me, madame. (*He grasps the dish and weaves towards the table*)
Aunt Marie Thank you. Please set it down by——
George (*quickly*) —I'll take it! (*He does so*)
Aunt Marie Very well. Set it down in front of——
Aramis (*loudly*) —Here we are! (*He sits at the table*)
Aunt Marie A small helping for me, Seraphine.
Raymond Seraphine?

George and Aramis leap up, pounce on Raymond and pull him upstage

(*Resisting*) That's not Sera——

George and Aramis clap their hands over Raymond's mouth

George Good-day, Raymond! See you tomorrow!
Aunt Marie (*ignoring the scuffle*) Now isn't this cream good? You must make your wife beat it longer, George. See, try it for yourself, Seraphine.
Raymond George! Don't tell me I am going mad!
George Yes, yes. Goodbye!
Raymond Hold on! Hey!

George and Aramis propel Raymond, struggling and protesting, out of the door

Raymond finally lurches off

George Goodbye, old fellow! (*To Aunt Marie*) What a character!
Aunt Marie One of France's alchoholic problems, I presume.
George Yes, yes. You see how one has to humour him.
Yvette I'll make the coffee.

Yvette exits into the kitchen

Aramis (*sitting*) There is an amusing story about how a fivepenny——
Aunt Marie (*rising*) I'll help you, Seraphine!
George No, Auntie, stay here. Aramis can tell you more about his collection.
Aunt Marie No, George! I'd like to help with the coffee. And I am quite sure Mr Aramis is quite exhausted! (*Bitterly*) You've kept him talking the whole lunchtime, poor man.

Aunt Marie exits into the kitchen

Aramis (*following Aunt Marie, with plates*) I did my best, George. Let's hope we have coffee in peace.
George You were wonderful, Aramis. I can never thank you! (*He begins to tidy up*)

Aramis exits into the kitchen

Seraphine enters upstage, with a suitcase

George Yes, madam, and what can I do — Oh! Seraphine!

Seraphine (*icily*) yes, 'Seraphine'! And Seraphine's had enough of all this I can tell you. (*She bangs down her case* DR)

George Huh! Don't imagine you're the only one!

Seraphine Get that woman out of my house!

George How can I do that now! What would I say to Aunt Marie?

Seraphine That's your affair.

George Seraphine! Remember our expectations.

Seraphine I don't care a button! This is my house and I'm staying here!

George Oh! We must talk this over. Please! Let's step down into the cellar out of sight for a moment. (*He guides her across* L)

Seraphine There's nothing to——

George Please! Just while we decide how we can get rid of them.

Seraphine Oh, all right.

Seraphine exits into the cellar

(*Off*) I'll tell you what you can do, you——

George slams the door to and bolts it

George Phew!

Aramis enters from the kitchen

(*Hissing frantically*) Aramis! Aramis!

Aramis What is it, George?

George Seraphine's here! She's in the cellar — until I've explained to Aunt Marie.

Aramis (*crossing to* C) The cellar! How did you pursuade her to do that?

George I shut her in.

Aramis (*wincing*) George! Oh, George that's really not the way.

There is a heavy thumping on the cellar door

George (*calling*) Forgive me, Seraphine! Forgive me, dearest! And do stop that infernal racket!

The racket stops

Aramis Thank heavens! She's quite safe down there, George?

George Yes, quite. The chute door is bolted.

Aramis That wasn't quite what I meant.

George At least. I think the chute door is bolted. Oh well…

Aramis (*moving to George*) Who but you, George, could complicate a simple situation so effectively.

George   Simple situation! Can't you see my position is utterly intolerable?

Aramis Then there is nothing for it — you must confess everything to your aunt and take a chance on her disinheriting you.

George Oh no!

Aramis Well, I've done my best for you (*He crosses* R)

George Oh, you have, dear friend, don't think I'll forget it.

Raymond enters behind George and Aramis. He creeps up to George, startling him

Raymond (*accusingly*) what have you done with Seraphine? Eh?

George I haven't done anything! That is — go away, will you!

Raymond   You're hiding something. I've read things like this. The wife's mouldering skeleton turns up years after — in the cellar.

George No, no, no! What a thought! (*He glances uneasily towards the cellar door*)

Aunt Marie (*off*) Coffee's ready!

Aramis George! Here comes your aunt!

George Oh dear! Wouldn't you think she'd lie down after that meal. The old are so energetic!

Raymond I know when people aren't telling the truth. It's written all over your face. All over it.

George (*desperately*) Why don't you look in the cellar for yourself! Here!

George guides Raymond towards the cupboard and opens the door

Raymond All right, I will — but don't think you're getting away with it because——

George thrusts Raymond into the cupboard and closes the door and locks it. There is the sound of Raymond collapsing among the brooms

Aramis George, what are you doing? One in the cellar and one in the cupboard…!

George What else can I do?

Aunt Marie enters with the coffee tray

Aunt Marie (*crossing to* C) George, I just saw a most curious individual climbing out of the cellar at the back of the house.
George (*to himself*) The chute door was not bolted.
Aunt Marie Who was it, George?
Aramis Didn't she say?
Aunt Marie No, she didn't speak. Seemed too dazed.
George Oh, she's the woman who cleans here, you know.
Aramis That's true anyway.
Aunt Marie Indeed? Doesn't look any too good-tempered, I must say.
George Oh, she is, I assure you. In the normal way. But right now she's troubled in her mind.
Aunt Marie Poor soul. What was she doing in the cellar?
George Er — cleaning — you know.
Aunt Marie In the cellar?
George Yes, yes, you see how industrious she is!
Aunt Marie Mm.
Seraphine (*off*) George!
Aramis Here she comes, George! (*He hurries to the arch*)
George Oh! Well, you run along and sit outside the café, Auntie. The afternoon air is very sweet here.
Aunt Marie What's the hurry, George?
George You don't want to miss it, do you?
Aunt Marie They switch it off? Very well, I'll go. I shall talk to those two charming foreigners.
George Yes, yes do!

Aunt Marie goes outside U *and joins the Foreigners*

Oh, Aramis, I don't think I can——

Seraphine enters from the kitchen, pushes Aramis aside and makes for George

Seraphine Ha! There you are, you slug!
George Now Seraphine... (*He guides her* D)
Seraphine This is the end! Where is Yvette?

Yvette enters from kitchen, pushing Aramis aside

Yvette Here is Yvette! And I couldn't agree more!
Seraphine You want to go?

Yvette (*moving* C) I can't wait to get out of this domestic paradise!

Seraphine   And I wouldn't set foot again in that upholstered rabbit hutch if you paid me!

Aramis   Well, at least the ladies recognize that they were better off as they were.

Seraphine   George and his wild ideas! Change places indeed.

George   (*sadly*) It didn't work out, did it? And now we are back as we were. Or will be as soon as Aunt Marie goes.

Seraphine   No! We change back right now!

Yvette   Right now!

Seraphine and Yvette pursue George and pin him against the cellar door

George   Aramis, don't just stand there! What am I to do?

Aramis   It was only to be expected, George. You know — the Chinese symbol for strife — two women under the same roof.

George   (*breaking away and running at Aramis*) I didn't want them under the same roof!

Aramis   Oh George, George, will you never learn.

The cupboard door bursts open and Raymond tumbles out. He sees Seraphine and clutches at her

Raymond   Seraphine! You're not dead! Thank God!

Seraphine   That's very kind, Raymond——

George   Raymond, please, as if——

Raymond   Your're alive! You're not under the patio!

Seraphine   Thank you for your concern, Raymond.

Aramis   He's very emotional.

George   He's very drunk.

Raymond   I'm so glad you're not dead. I'm so glad you're alive.

Seraphine   Oh do shut up, Raymond.

Raymond   I'll tell everyone you're back. That you're not dead after all! (*He makes for the door*)

George   No please, Raymond. Don't tell everyone—at least not out that way.

Raymond   I thought you were dead! I told everyone.

George   Oh heavens!

Aramis   What a terrible shock for you, Raymond.

Raymond   I must let everyone know you're not dead.

Aramis   Oh, you must! At once. Come along, out the back way.

Aramis starts to guide Raymond off stage, into the kitchen

Raymond Where are we going?
Aramis It's a short cut.

Aramis and Raymond exit

Raymond (*off*) I'm so glad she's not dead!
Yvette (*crossing to the bar*) I'm going to pack!
George No!
Seraphine Good. I'm going to unpack!
George Seraphine! Yvette! Wait until Auntie goes!
Seraphine } (*together*) No!
Yvette
George But how am I going to explain to the old——

Aunt Marie enters

Aunt Marie George——
George Er — ha ha, hallo, Auntie——
Aunt Marie George, I want to talk to you.
George Well, of course, Auntie. Do sit down. (*Hissing*) For heaven's sake keep quiet now, Seraphine—and you, Yvette! (*Indicating Seraphine*) Auntie, this is—er—er—Yvette's mother!

Seraphine drops her case

Aunt Marie It's all right, George, you needn't dissemble any longer.
George Auntie! Why, I—I—you *know*?

George, Aramis, Seraphine and Yvette all gather round Aunt Marie

Aunt Marie I've just asked the couple sitting outside and they've confirmed my suspicion. This is your wife and not Yvette here.
George (*bitterly*) I told you they were picking up the language!
Aunt Marie (*sitting upstage of the table* LC) Now then, George, why have you practised this deceit upon me? Who is this Yvette anyway?
Aramis She is George's—er—a friend of the family.
George Yes, a friend of the family.
Seraphine Yes. George sees her rather more frequently than I but she is a friend of the family.
Aunt Marie Mm. Yes. I think that makes it perfectly plain.

George (*wearily*) It used to be simple enough.

Aunt Marie But what was Yvette doing here running the house when I arrived?

George It was like this, Auntie. Both Seraphine and Yvette had become completely bored and irritated with their respective situations— and we thought it would please them to swap over for a month.

Aunt Marie And did it?

Yvette ⎫
Seraphine ⎭ (*together*) No!

George I'm afraid they seemed even less contented than before.

Aunt Marie Of course they did. Really, George, you have no understanding of women at all.

Aramis Just what I told him, madam.

Aunt Marie You've gone about the whole thing the wrong way.

Aramis My very words!

George What else could I do to give them a change? Send them away?

Aunt Marie Not necessary.

George What then?

Aunt Marie Send yourself away!

George What?

Aunt Marie (*rising*) It's obvious to a child of two—it's you they are tired of George—you!

George Do you really think so?

Aunt Marie Of course they are! And who wouldn't be! George, you must take a holiday and let some other man take them over for a while.

Yvette ⎫
Seraphine ⎭ (*together*) Oh yes!

George You needn't sound quite so thrilled! Anyway who—for goodness' sake?

Aramis starts for the door—quietly

Aunt Marie Obviously, it's the sort of task a man could only trust to his best friend. The sort of job that—where are you going, Mr Aramis?

Aramis I was just—er——

George and Aunt Marie move up either on side of Aramis

George Aramis! Of course! Aramis, I've just had a splendid notion!

Aramis George!

George And you're on leave too! What a happy coincidence.

Aunt Marie Well, girls, will Aramis do? Remember a change is as good as a tonic.

Seraphine and Yvette whisper together

Seraphine ⎫
Yvette ⎭ *(together)* He'll do!

Aramis But—but——

George Oh, Aramis, what a friend you are! Here, take my apron—
clean this morning! Of course you know where everything is—how
fortunate!

*Aunt Marie ties the apron round Aramis. George gets his tie from the
pegs*

Aramis *(frantically)* But, George, you can't—I mean—how can you
trust your womenfolk with me. I mean, a man of my reputation!

George My dear Aramis, I want them to have only the best! (*He goes
DL to the mirror*)

Aramis *(pathetically)* But, George—I have bought my ticket to
Boulogne.

Aunt Marie Splendid! George has a cousin in Boulogne. He can stay
with her. Do you remember her, George?

George *(putting on his tie)* Yes, Auntie. Didn't she have red hair?

Aunt Marie And green eyes, George. Green.

Aunt Marie goes upstairs

George I'll buy the ticket off you, of course, Aramis.

Aramis *(sitting U of the table LC; brokenly)* It doesn't matter.

George No, no, as you said, it leads to embarrassment. Here! (*He pays
Aramis*)

Aramis Embarrassment!

George What time did you say the train left?

Aramis Two-thirty.

George Good gracious, I've only a few minutes to catch it—and I've
not packed! Aramis, I suppose you wouldn't consider?

Aramis Take it! (*He passes over the case*)

George Oh, thank you. I must fly! Goodbye, Seraphine! You'll explain
to the police about not being dead won't you? (*Kissing Seraphine on
both cheeks*) Cooperate with Aramis, won't you, my dear.

Seraphine *(moving to Aramis' left side)* Oh, most certainly I will!

Aramis Oh!

George You too, Yvette. (*He kisses her cheeks*)

Yvette Don't you worry about that! (*She moves to Aramis' right side*)

Aramis *(apprehensively)* George!

George Goodbye, Aramis! I wouldn't leave them with anyone else, you know, but a man of your experience. (*Shaking Aramis' hands*) What a friend!

Aunt Marie comes downstairs wearing her hat

Aunt Marie I'm coming too, George. You'll find my case packed and ready on the landing.

George darts upstairs to get it

Aunt Marie (*shaking hands with each*) Goodbye, Seraphine! Yvette. Goodbye, Mr Aramis—so interesting—your stamp collection.

Aramis rises and is firmly reseated by the girls

George comes downstairs with Aunt Marie's case

George Here! We'll walk down to the station together.
Aunt Marie (*putting on her gloves*) I shall get a few presents to take home on the way.
George That's the idea.

George and Aunt Marie move towards the door

Aramis (*supplicating*) George—come back!
George Goodbye!
Aunt Marie I can get something from that foreign couple sitting outside—selling brushes!

Aunt Marie and George turn and set off arm-in-arm

Yvette and Seraphine close in on Aramis

CURTAIN

FURNITURE AND PROPERTY LIST

ACT I
SCENE 1

On stage: Bar. *On it:* radio, plate, sugar-bowl, bottles, a small glass, tea-
towel, tray with two wine glasses and an open bottle of wine
A few tables and chairs
Door and window shutters
Cupboard. *In it:* mop, several brushes
Coat-pegs. *On them:* George's tie, George's coat
Mirror on the wall

Off stage: Tea-towel (**Seraphine**)
Bottles of wine (**George**)
Case, walking stick, paper bag of edible pastries (**Aramis**)
Bucket (**Seraphine**)
Cup/tray of coffee (**Seraphine**)
Tray with two cups of coffee and a plate of pastries (**Seraphine**)
Newspaper (**Raymond**)
Shawl (**Seraphine**)
Brooms and brushes (**Foreigners**)

Personal: **Aramis**: three postage stamps in small, transparent envelopes,
small magnifying glass
George: small magnifying glass, bank-notes
Foreigners: money

SCENE 2

On stage: As Scene 1

Set: Bar. *On it*: Cruet bottles, vase of flowers, champagne and two
glasses
Cupboard. *In it:* camp bed, mattress, rug

Off stage: Brooms and brushes (**Foreigners**)
Hat, box of chocolates, a little jewel box, cushions (**George**)

Personal: **Female Foreigner**: money

ACT II
SCENE 1

Re-set: Shutters open

Strike: Camp bed, mattress, rug, champagne and glasses, Seraphine's
               coat

Set: Bar. *Under it*: Sugar *On it*; Duster
               Two glasses on the outside table

Off stage: Brooms and brushes (**Foreigners**)
               Two cups of coffee (**George**)
               Small suitcase (**Aunt Marie**)

Personal: **Aramis**: watch

SCENE 2

Re-set: George's tie on the pegs

Strike: Coffee cups, small suitcase, sugar

Set: Table. *On it*; Cutlery, plates and cruet
               Bar. *On it*; Dirty cloth, two bottles of wine, wine glasses. *Under it*;
               Sewing basket

Off stage: Chair cover (**Aunt Marie**)
               Bottles (**George**)
               Suitcase (**Aramis**)
               Casserole and plates (**George** and **Aramis**)
               Newspaper (**Aramis**)
               Plate of tomatoes (**George**)
               Large flan (**Aunt Marie**)
               Suitcase (**Seraphine**)
               Tray of coffee (**Aunt Marie**)
               Hat (**Aunt Marie**)
               Suitcase (**George**)

Personal: **George**: money
               Aunt Marie: gloves

LIGHTING PLOT

Property fittings required: nil
One interior set

ACT I, Scene 1

To open: Bright general interior lighting

Cue 1	**George** and **Aramis** drink	(Page 24)
	Fade to Black-out	

ACT I, Scene 2

To open: Bright general interior lighting, late evening lighting outside

Cue 2	**George** goes through the arch	(Page 29)
	The lights go down	
Cue 3	**George** and **Seraphine** sleep peacefully	(Page 34)
	Fade to Black-out	

ACT II, Scene 1

To open: Bright general interior lighting

Cue 4	**George, Yvette** and **Aramis** slowly rise	(Page 44)
	Fade to Black-out	

ACT II, Scene 2

To open: Bright general interior lighting

Cue 5	**Yvette** and **Seraphine** close in on **Aramis**	(Page 65)
	Rapid fade as the Curtain *closes*	

EFFECTS PLOT
ACT I

Use of Copyright Music